A LAST REQUEST
THAT WAS JUST
THE BEGINNING . . .

At the age of twelve, Danny Sugerman was a restless Los Angeles youth sitting on a powder keg of pent-up energy, looking for a direction and a hero. He found both in Jim Morrison, the brilliant but tormented leader of the Doors. Sugerman, quickly drawn in as employee, friend and confidant, later found out that meeting Morrison was no accident. Centuries ago Morrison was a dying abbot who wanted to leave his sacred books under Sugerman's charge. The teachings they contained included the use of drugs for spiritual enlightenment. But Sugerman, a young pupil in that life, felt unprepared for the task and fled the monastery. To make up for refusing the dying abbot's final request, Sugerman assumed management of the Doors' catalogue after Morrison's death, fought his own war with heroin addiction and has written two books of his own, including Morrison's biography.

ROSEMARY ELLEN GUILEY is a journalist and author of several works on psychic phenomena. She is a member of the American Society of Psychical Research and the Association of Research and Enlightenment.

TALES OF
REINCARNATION

ROSEMARY ELLEN GUILEY

POCKET BOOKS

New York   London   Toronto   Sydney   Tokyo

An *Original* Publication of POCKET BOOKS

POCKET BOOKS, a division of Simon & Schuster Inc.
1230 Avenue of the Americas, New York, NY 10020

ISBN: 0-671-66257-0

First Pocket Books printing October 1989

10 9 8 7 6 5 4 3 2 1

POCKET and colophon are trademarks of
Simon & Schuster Inc.

Printed in the U.S.A.

For Olga Vezeris

ACKNOWLEDGMENTS

I would like to express my deep gratitude to the individuals who granted interviews to share their expertise and experiences for this book, including Alexandria, Andorian, Annie B., Gail Bartley, Marion Zimmer Bradley, Barbara Hand Clow, Selena Fox, Pamela Glasser, Doug Hobart, Craig Junjulas, Lynn L., Sandee Mac, Laurie McQuary, Ornyece Prince, Danny Sugerman, Alice T., Michael Talbot, "Pat," "Kerry," "Bill," "Tom R.," and a number of others who shared their stories but wished to remain anonymous. I would also like to thank Professor V. V. Akolkar, parapsychologist, of Pune, India, for allowing me to read his unpublished report on the case of "Sharada" and cite some of his conclusions. Thanks to all of you for your contributions. I would like to add a special thanks to Barbara Hand Clow, Sandee Mac, Laurie McQuary, Michael Talbot, and Alice T., who opened other doors for me.

Finally, I would like to thank my editor, Claire Zion, who conceived the idea for this book and offered me the opportunity to execute it.

CONTENTS

INTRODUCTION

Tales of Reincarnation is a collection of the stories of a wide range of individuals who have encountered themselves in past-life recall. The stories, most of them from contemporary people in all walks of life, are full of surprises, drama, tragedy, happiness, discovery, and revelation.

The purpose of this book is to look at the impact of past-life recall: When confronted with information or memories that appear to be related to another life in another time, how does one's perspective of self, the world, and the cosmos change? As the stories here demonstrate, the change is often positive, ranging from a shift in attitude to a complete transformation in lifestyle and purpose.

I am not attempting here to prove the validity of reincarnation. The experiences herein speak for themselves, and readers may draw their own conclusions. The individuals included express a range of attitudes toward reincarnation from skepticism to acceptance. Regardless, all found meaning in their experiences, and that is the important result.

TALES OF
REINCARNATION

CHAPTER ONE

Reincarnation in the Age of New Consciousness

The door to the past sometimes swings open unexpectedly. When it does, strange winds blow through our lives, bringing bits and pieces from unknown lands in unknown times that swirl 'round us, teasing and mystifying. Oddly, we know that these bits and pieces belong to us. Looking through the open door into an endless dark, we are suddenly aware that the immediate physical world in which we are rooted is no longer All There Is. We feel extensions of ourselves out there in the dark, essences waiting to take on form.

A glimpse through the door to the past can challenge our fundamental beliefs about life, death, and the fate of the soul upon death. If we do not believe in reincarnation yet are confronted with an experience that convinces us we have lived before, then we must reevaluate our role in the scheme of the cosmos. If the experience has any meaning for us at all, our lives invariably change, and usually for the better.

The interest in exploring past lives is part of the Age of New Consciousness, the movement that began in the 1960s to explore metaphysical, spiritual, religious, and holistic systems and concepts. I believe the term "Age of New Consciousness" best describes what this movement is about, far more so than "Age of Aquarius" or "New Age." Those of us who are influenced by the Age of New Consciousness are searching for ways to expand and uplift our consciousness, to see the cosmos and our role in it from new perspectives. Looking at past lives is one of those ways.

Since the 1960s, an increasing number of Westerners have embarked upon past-life journeys to discover themselves or solve problems by undergoing regression by hypnosis. Many persons have sought past-life therapy from practitioners of this relatively new profession.

For some individuals, however, the journey into the past begins unexpectedly, when the door to the past suddenly swings open and they dare to step through to the other side.

FROM MASADA YOU CAN SEE FOREVER

The ruins of Masada, the ancient fortress where the Jews made their final, desperate stand against the invading Romans in A.D. 70, sit atop a dry, boat-shaped mountain in southeast Israel. More than 1,400 feet below lies the southwest shore of the Dead Sea. Masada, which may have been settled as early as 900 B.C., reached its peak in glory under the rule of Herod the Great, king of Judaea under the Romans from 37 to 4 B.C. Herod built palaces, huge walls, aqueducts, and water cisterns there. Following his death in 4 B.C., the Romans took Masada, but lost it in A.D. 66 to Jewish Zealots who opposed Roman dominion. The Romans attacked again, and in A.D. 70 destroyed the

Temple in the city of Jerusalem, which fell to them.

A band of 1,000 Zealots refused to surrender. The men, women, and children took refuge in Masada, and held off 15,000 Roman soldiers for more than two years. The Romans finally breached the fortress by building a slope up to the wooden walls and setting them afire. Inside, they found that the Zealots had committed mass suicide rather than be taken captive. Only seven women and children, who hid in an aqueduct, survived.

For Pamela Glasser, a young musician from Texas, the first inkling that she had lived before came in a startling déjà vu experience at Masada in May 1986 during Passover. Glasser, a French horn player, was spending a year with an orchestra in Israel. Of mixed ancestry and raised a Catholic, she did not consider herself particularly religious and knew only a little about Judaism and the history of the Hebrew people. Yet she felt strangely at home in Israel, as though she had returned to familiar and comfortable surroundings. During her visit to Masada, a popular tourist attraction, that feeling of familiarity became a catalyst for a journey into the past. Here is Glasser's account:

> I was climbing the Snake Path of Masada. When I was about halfway up, I had a strong, visual flash of a covered earthen vase. It was a simple clay pot with a top. Immediately after I turned a curve in the path, I saw a niche in the rock with a flat shelf, and I knew that the vase had been there at one time, and that it had held water. The niche was a water stop. It was an eerie feeling.
>
> I continued up the path. When I got to the top, I looked out over the ruins. It was a pretty, bright day, and everything looked sparkly. I went to the edge farthest from the Dead Sea, and as I looked down the slope that the Romans had built, I felt a

great tightness in my entire abdomen area, and strong anger. I had a flash of soldiers swarming up the slope. I felt both anger and grief. I felt that I had been up there in the fortress and had taken my own life and the lives of my family. It was quite an unexpected and very emotional experience.

Glasser mentioned her experience to several persons, but was dismayed when they failed to grasp the emotional significance of it for her. "Interesting," they commented. Nonetheless, the memory of it burned in her mind. It was still fresh when she returned to the States a few months later.

She began to wonder if there was truth to the concept of reincarnation, about which she knew little. Her Catholic faith certainly did not endorse it. Some of her friends believed in it, but she felt ambivalent.

The déjà vu at Masada haunted her. Finally, Glasser mentioned her experience to her horn instructor, who referred her to Sandee Mac, a past-life hypnotherapist in Houston. Glasser underwent a series of hypnotic regressions that, as she put it, "turned up a lot of surprises." Each past life offered a lesson for her to apply to her present life.

In the first session, she returned to the life that had ended at Masada, and saw herself as a forty-year-old man, a Zealot soldier named Ilan. Ilan and his two sons, ages nineteen and twenty, fought fiercely against the Romans and sacrificed themselves when they saw the end was at hand, Glasser said.

The important lesson for me to learn from this life was that I was still carrying a lot of anger that had to be resolved. I also had to learn to forgive myself for committing suicide and to forgive the Romans for what they did. I had to be able to take a higher view of the whole situation, see the sweep of history. That was far more important than my personal feelings of anger. As a result, I resolved a lot of resentment that I had in this lifetime for authority figures, which I think related to that life.

Since then, it's been easier for me to work with others, especially if they're giving me instructions. I used to resist taking directions. Now when I work with a conductor, it's much easier for me to accept what the conductor says and just do it.

Because of Glasser's affinity with Israel, Mac suggested looking at other past lives in that part of the world. One life that surfaced struck Glasser as "bizarre," but had a tremendous impact upon her and shifted her professional focus:

I was a person called Aella, a woman, and I lived in Atlantis near the end before it sank. I worked in a pyramid-shaped healing center to help people who had deformities, like missing or extra limbs. Inside the healing temple were huge granite baths that had grills or grates inside them. The baths were filled to just above the grate line. Under the water below the grates were amethyst clusters. Patients would lie in the water on top of the grates and go into a meditative state. I would either sing or play a type of stringed instrument that somehow vibrated the grate and the water. Incredible cures happened. People who were missing limbs would grow new ones after several treatments.

Before Atlantis sank, I moved on into Egypt, where I did not feel at home at all in the culture. I went off with some followers into the Sinai area, where we found a valley with a subterranean cavern. There were four entrances to the cavern, which was almost pyramidal in shape. We reconstructed pretty much what had been in the Atlantean healing temple. I felt we had some help from alien beings in doing the grates, which were made out of a strange metal, something like titanium.

The life was bizarre to me because I didn't know very much about Atlantis and didn't even know what amethyst was, other than a crystal. I knew that pyramids supposedly have some kind of power, although I didn't necessarily believe it at the time I was doing the hypnosis.

I feel very strongly that the cavern is still in existence somewhere in the Sinai. The entrances are probably under sand, but I think they could be excavated.

Aella's lifetime also is affecting my lifetime now. I've become more interested in healing, especially in techniques to combine sound and crystals. It also opened up a chakra point, a sensitivity, in my hands, and I have stopped headaches and such. I've never been trained in massage therapy, but now, using my hands, I can locate points on the body, including the feet, that throb and pulsate. I work with these spots, and then the headache or whatever is gone. People say my hands get very hot, but I don't feel the heat myself.

Glasser said she did not intend to become a touch healer, however, because the direction of her healing work lay in music and crystals. She began to study how music and sound affect the mind and body, and how to use music and sound in healing. She discovered, for example, that Baroque pieces, especially played on the flute or recorder, stimulate the intellect. Various instruments seem to affect different chakras, she said: the flute stimulates the crown chakra while the French horn stimulates the heart.

Glasser also has pursued study of "crystal energetics," the healing properties of crystals, and the mysterious power of pyramids. With others, she began constructing a small pyramid healing chamber, modeled after the Great Pyramid and built to scale with a gold capstone. Glasser's role was to develop crystal gridworks and select a music library for use in the chamber.

Other past lifetimes explored by Glasser revealed her karmic ties to family members and other persons in her present life. Glasser had suffered a traumatic childhood and the early death of her father. One past life helped her to heal old wounds:

When I was two [in the present life], my father died of cancer. My mother told me later that she took me to see him right before he died and that I had a fit in the hospital. I was emotionally scarred by his death. I had a pretty rough childhood, problems with thumb-sucking until I was six and bed-wetting until I was nine. My mother remarried, but I don't have any recollections of getting along with my stepfather.

[As an adult] I've had a lot of relationships with men and none of them seemed to work out very well. I've often looked for a father figure. I thought it would be a good idea to check this out in past lives.

I found out that I've been connected to my father in many, many lifetimes. The most important one was in Druid times, long ago in Britain, in an area that is now northwestern England. We lived out in the woods. My father was a religious leader of our group. I played a flute and worked closely with him. I got so involved in going off on my own into the woods to play the flute and converse with birds that I had a hard time getting along with people. I was very close to my father— too close, probably, that was the lesson there— and when he died I completely withdrew. I had married someone because I was instructed that I had to. He was somebody I used to be involved with romantically in this lifetime. In this life, he withdrew from me the way I had withdrawn from him in that life. I saw the karmic relationship there, and it helped me to understand what had happened between us.

I also realized that when I was born in this lifetime, I expected to have once again that really good closeness with my father. My lesson was to learn to live without him and to get more involved with people. Seeing my Druid life also helped me get back in touch with my love of nature, and I'm really grateful for that. I'm getting involved in saving trees and critters, as well as learning to like people again. It's been a really beneficial thing to go through.

The other past lives I saw dealt with karmic issues concerning family and boyfriends. What I'd like to say about them is that they have brought a great deal of healing, and have helped me get along much better with my mother. I have not had a past life with my stepfather that I can recall, but I get along better with him, having learned that he did not replace my father and put him out of my life. I now have a boyfriend with whom I'm getting along quite well. We are learning a lot from each other and having a good time doing it.

Overall, going through these past-life regressions has opened me up. My music means a lot more to me. I've always loved music, but it's been a selfish love. Now I'm learning that it helps others. Performing has become more important to me, not just for my own sake but for the sake of the audience as well. Formerly, I just wanted to play and make money doing it. Money is still important—I have bills to pay, of course—but I do more for free and more for children. Reaching children is a beautiful experience. I joined a woodwind quintet that does concerts for young audiences. And I teach privately and I'm enjoying that much more. Even if none of my students become horn players professionally, the experience is great.

The experience in Israel made me start thinking that reincarnation is real. If not, maybe there exists some kind of collective unconscious, as Jung put it, and somehow our minds can tie into it and see these experiences. I'm comfortable with either explanation. I see the value of doing regression work, because it has helped me in this lifetime. It probably could help others as well.

Glasser's experience is not an uncommon one. An experience—a flash of déjà vu, a vivid dream, a conversation with a friend, a particularly thought-provoking book—stimulates the desire to find out if and how we lived before. The exploration is never dull, but full of surprises, revelations, often intense emotions, and insights that can lead to change and growth. There is something rich to be learned from even the most humdrum past life.

WHO BELIEVES IN REINCARNATION?

Most of the world's population believes in some form of reincarnation or rebirth, in which the soul returns to earth to inhabit another body as part of a spiritual evolution or ongoing cosmic cycle. In the predominantly Christian West, belief in reincarnation is not widespread, but there are indications that more people are discovering it, at least in some areas. A 1969 Gallup poll of twelve Western nations found belief among the adult populations to range from a low of 10 percent in the Netherlands to a high of 26 percent in Canada; Great Britain and the United States fell in the upper two-thirds at 18 percent and 20 percent respectively. In 1981, a Gallup survey of the United States showed that 23 percent believed in reincarnation, nearly one-fourth of all adults in the country. More women were believers (25 percent of those polled) than men (21 percent). In terms of Christian denominations, Methodists ranked the highest with 26 percent, followed by Catholics at 25 percent, Lutherans at 22 percent, and Protestants at 21 percent.

It is likely that the number of reincarnation believers has continued to rise. The Age of New Consciousness came into full bloom in the 1980s, bringing many people into contact with a wide range of metaphysical and spiritual doctrines and concepts. Past-life regression, the act of examining past lives while under hypnosis, became more commonplace, and also gained acceptance as an alternative therapy tool. The 1980s also saw the success of actress Shirley MacLaine in her revelations about her personal past-life odysseys. MacLaine made it acceptable to millions of people not only to explore and speak about such concepts, but to consider them as possible truths. Other individuals who have brought the idea of reincarnation to large audiences are Dick Sutphen, of Malibu, California, who began giving regression seminars in the 1970s, and author Ruth Montgomery. These individuals have all built upon the work of Madame Helena P. Blavatsky, who helped introduce Eastern thought to the West through theosophy beginning in the late nineteenth century, and on the work of Edgar Cayce, one of America's best-known psychics, who could accurately diagnose illnesses and prescribe remedies while in trance. Cayce, who died in 1945, began talking about karma and the influence of past lives as early as 1923. His thousands of readings continue to be cited as authoritative sources on reincarnation and a wide range of other subjects.

THE DOCTRINE OF REINCARNATION

Reincarnation is a complex doctrine with many variations and subtleties and a long history. A brief summary is given here. Readers who wish to explore the subject in more depth will find excellent sources listed in the bibliography at the end of this volume.

The modern West derives its idea of reincarnation from the Hindu and Buddhist religions. The Buddhist concepts of reincarnation are derived from Hinduism, though there are some significant differences between the two faiths.

According to this doctrine, the soul is imperfect when it first comes into the world, and only perfects itself through a series of incarnations, beginning with the mineral kingdom and moving up through the plant kingdom, animal kingdom, and finally into the human realm. In each kingdom, the soul begins at the lowest level of consciousness and must advance to the highest level possible in that realm before it can reach the next kingdom. In the human kingdom, the soul begins in the bodies of persons preoccupied with gratifying the senses. It then advances to an intellectual level, and finally to a spiritual level, where the personality pursues enlightenment through meditation, study, and contemplation rather than in lower material ways. In Hinduism, the goal of the soul is to be reunited with

Brahman, the ultimate reality of the universe. When that happens, the need to reincarnate ceases.

Dharma is the law or truth that governs the operation of the entire universe. In terms of the physical world, the most important aspects of *dharma* are *samsara*, or reincarnation; *karma*, the law of cause and effect; and *moksha*, or spiritual liberation. Reincarnation is governed by karma, which says in essence that we reap what we sow. One's pain and joy, success and failure, beauty and ugliness, indeed, all aspects of life, are the result of karma. Good thoughts and acts are rewarded in future lives with spiritual advancement; evil thoughts and acts are punished by regression, including incarnations as lower forms of life. *Moksha* is the release of the soul from reincarnation through realization of the self, which is the merging with Brahman. In the Hindu view, the personality remains intact throughout its many lives. In the Hindu sacred writings, there are merely inferences of rebirth or reincarnation in the oldest works, known collectively as the Vedas (Sanskrit for "knowledge"), most of which date to around 1200 B.C. and which consist of four collections of mantras, chants, hymns, rituals, and prayers. The *Upanishads* (meaning "sitting at the master's feet"), a collection of philosophical scriptures composed around 800-700 B.C. that form the final section of the Veda, deal primarily with self-realization; they also contain references to reincarnation. The doctrines of reincarnation and karma are explained in the *Bhagavad-Gita* ("The Lord's Song"), part of the epic poem the *Mahabharata* ("Great Bharata"), written between 400 B.C. and A.D. 200 (though according to some scholars, it is pre-Buddhist and dates to the sixth century B.C.).

In Buddhism, the soul also goes through a series of lives, the circumstances of which are governed by the law of karma. The Pali Canon, the early Buddhist scriptures, shows that Buddha taught that the individual has a lesser self, which dies with the body, and a greater self, which survives.

Modern Buddhists, however, believe that the personality does not remain intact from life to life. Instead, they embrace the concept of *anatta*, "no-self" or "non-self." At death, the personality disintegrates into sparks or pieces that mix with other pieces and coalesce into a new personality. It is only the life-force, the will to live, that survives, like one candle lighting another.

Furthermore, Buddhists reject the concept of Brahman as the ultimate reality. The end goal of reincarnation is *nirvana*, or enlightenment. The highest level of nirvana is Buddhahood, in which all ego, desire, and ignorance are extinguished. Nirvana, meaning "extinction," is a state of ineffable happiness and peace, free of reincarnation. There is disagreement between the two major schools of Buddhism, Theravada and Mahayana, as to whether Buddha himself attained nirvana. In the Theravada view, he did; the Mahayana view asserts that at the threshold of nirvana, Buddha vowed never to cross it as long as there were suffering beings on the earth still in the wheel of rebirth.

Both Hindus and Buddhists view reincarnation as misery, suffering, sorrow, and illusion. All acts of bad karma bind one to the wheel of rebirth, which means more misery. Reincarnation is something from which to escape.

There are different kinds of karma. Karma of the body includes one's gestures and physical acts, such as hugs, blows, building, destroying, nurturing, killing. Karma of the mouth concerns one's words. Karma of the mind concerns one's thoughts. Thus, with each thought, word, and deed, we create karma. The *Mahabharata* states, "Just as a calf finds out its mother among a thousand cows, so also an action that was performed in a previous birth follows the doer." Both Hindu and Buddhist faiths teach that the individual is his or her own master, and is completely responsible for his or her karma.

Both Hindus and Buddhists believe that humans may reincarnate in nonhuman forms, such as animals, an event dictated by karma. In Buddhism, reincarnation occurs in a wheel of rebirth that has six regions: *devas* (gods), *asuras* (elemental forces), humans, animals, *pretas* (hungry ghosts)—a purgatory of unsatisfied desires, and hell, another temporary state of purgatory. Only the human realm offers the opportunity for awareness and enlightenment. Reincarnation revolves around the wheel, governed by karma, until ignorance and earthly cravings are overcome.

In Eastern doctrine, karma is literal in cause and effect, that is, an eye for an eye. It also is immutable and inescapable: once an act is committed, that act's karma must be balanced. According to some Eastern schools of thought, however, karma may be "worked off" through meditation, chanting mantras, and the like.

Reincarnation in the Middle East and the West

The ancient Egyptians believed in reincarnation, and in the transmigration of human souls into animal bodies, concepts probably learned from ancient India. The Egyptians at one time held that a soul might remain in an animal form for as long as 3,000 years before being able to return to human form. The earlier Egyptians believed reincarnation applied only to rulers; the doctrine eventually was extended to the masses.

The ancient Greeks had a concept called *metempsychosis,* which is the passage of a soul at death into another body, human or animal. This concept, received from the Egyptians, passed into the Orphic mysteries prior to the time of Pythagoras (about 582-507 B.C.). Pythagoras and later Plato (around 427-347 B.C.) were among the Greek philosophers who taught about reincarnation; Pythagoras is said to have remembered his previous lives and his times between lives. There is disagreement among scholars as to whether the two philosophers also taught metempsychosis in its literal sense. Some Platonists said that if a soul regressed to animal form, it did not actually become the soul of the animal, but rather took the animal over much like a *daimon,* (Greek for "divine power") which, in modern terms, is the approximate equivalent of a spirit guide or inner voice.

The Romans absorbed Greek thought and culture into their own, including the concept of reincarnation, but belief in it reached a low point by 44 B.C., when Julius Caesar was murdered.

Reincarnation is not part of Islam, Judaism, or Christianity, though sects of each religion do believe in it. The Sufis, the mystical sect of Islam whose members claim that it predates the prophet Mohammed (A.D. 570-632) by several thousand years, believe in it. In Judaism, reincarnation is the concept of *gilgul,* which has had various interpretations over the centuries. Reincarnation does not appear in the Torah, but does in the Kabbalah, the mystical teachings, which were first published in the thirteenth century but attributed to first century A.D. authors. According to the Kabbalah, early Jews believed that great prophets reincarnated, that Adam became David, who was to be the Messiah. The suffering of Job is interpreted by some as karma. From about the thirteenth century through the eighteenth century, one dominant concept held that Adam's soul scattered into sparks, which were being reassembled through reincarnation. The idea is very similar to the Buddhist concept.

Reincarnation is not taught by the three main branches of Judaism—Reform, Conservative, and Orthodox—but is by the Hasidim, a sect that teaches the mysteries of the Kabbalah.

The presence of reincarnation in Christianity has been the subject of great debate. Cayce perhaps summed it up best when he commented, "I can read reincarnation into the Bible, and you can read it right out again!" Reincarnationists interpret numerous passages from the Bible as evidence of the concept, while opponents cite the same passages and disagree. The idea of reincarnation was taught by the Essenes, a sect with which Jesus had contact. The Gnostics believed in a concept of karma and reincarnation. Origen (A.D. 185-254), a Christian theologian with Gnostic leanings, believed in the preexistence of the soul and reincarnation in a succession of bodies determined by the soul's merits and demerits. Origen's teachings were condemned as anathema in 553 by Emperor Justinian, the head of the Christian church. From that time on, belief in reincarnation withered in orthodox Christianity, but was kept alive by various sects and secret societies. Today, no mainstream denomination of Christianity teaches about reincarnation. The Unity Church, which has attracted many Age of New Consciousness followers, endorses the concept.

Reincarnation received renewed attention in the West during the nineteenth century with the rise of the Spiritualist and Theosophical movements. The Spiritualist movement was concerned largely with proving survival after death through mediumistic communications with the dead, and as the movement grew, it split on the issue of reincarnation. Most modern Spiritualists believe in the preexistence of the soul; some believe in a law of return like those in Eastern philosophies, while others feel free will is a determining factor in whether or not a soul reincarnates.

The Theosophical Society, founded in 1875 by Blavatsky, a Russian mystic, along with Colonel H. S. Olcott, William Q. Judge, and a small group of others, was instrumental in bringing the concept of reincarnation to a wider Western audience. In the Theosophists' view, however, reincarnation is endless, for the universe is endless.

Reincarnation Among Tribal Societies

Belief in reincarnation is widespread in tribal societies in the North, Central, and South Americas. Medicine men, shamans, and seers, who are initiated into the mysteries of death and birth, are the most likely individuals to hold reincarnation beliefs.

In North America, the Eskimo and Tlingit have strong reincarnation beliefs and customs. The Tlingit expect reincarnating souls to announce themselves beforehand in dreams, usually to the mother, but possibly to other family members. This act serves to identify the incoming spirit, usually a deceased member of the family, so that the child can be named appropriately (see Chapter Ten). The Eskimo believe that some souls may inhabit either human or animal bodies, while others inhabit only human forms. The Dakota hold that medicine men may be reborn four times. In between, they live in the spirit realm where the gods give them instruction in healing and magic. When they reincarnate, they remember these times. The Algonquin east of the Mississippi have a curious "reincarnation" rite in which outsiders may be adopted by families to replace deceased members of the household. The adoptee takes the dead person's name and is considered the reincarnation of that individual. Reincarnation beliefs also exist among the Winnebago (a Sioux tribe), Creek, Hopi, Mohave, Montagnais (an Algonquin tribe), Haida, Athabaskan, Aleut (an Eskimo tribe), Kiowa, Aht, and Gitskan.

The Iroquois believe in reincarnation of humans as animals.

In South America, reincarnation is widely held as a belief among numerous small tribes, as well as the Patagonia of Argentina, the Peruvian Indians, the Chiriquane of Brazil, and the Jivaro of Ecuador, the latter of whom believe humans reincarnate as animals and birds.

Elsewhere, reincarnation beliefs are held by tribal societies throughout Africa, Australia, and the Pacific Islands. In parts of Africa, it is believed that one perpetuates oneself by reincarnating through family lineage; childlessness is considered a curse because it hinders ancestors from returning. The idea of reincarnation prevails universally among the Australian Aborigines, the central tribes of whom believe they will come back as whites. Beliefs vary among Pacific Islanders. Okinawans, for example, believe the soul lingers in its former home for forty-nine days, then enters the spirit realm, where it spends an indeterminate amount of time before entering a new human form. The Huna belief system of Hawaii embraces an evolutionary spiral from the mineral kingdom up to the human kingdom.

Tribal reincarnation beliefs vary greatly around the world and have more differences than similarities. Some societies believe that humans return only as humans, and some restrict this even further to reincarnation only within families. Others believe humans return only in nonhuman forms, as animals, birds, insects, reptiles, fish, flowers, trees, and rocks. Still others believe humans reincarnate in either human or nonhuman form.

MODERN VIEWS OF REINCARNATION

Westerners who believe in reincarnation have adapted the concept to fit the prevailing beliefs of their society. Perhaps most significantly, Westerners look at reincarnation optimistically and do not view it as a wheel of misery, but as a wheel of growth, with the end result being reunion with God, or enlightenment in a spiritual state or plane of existence. Westerners believe strongly in free will and self-determinism. Therefore, the law of karma is not entirely immutable, as they see it, but may be affected by choices. It is believed that the individual *plans* the next life and *chooses* the circumstances in order to balance certain karmic forces. The planning is done by the Higher Self, which is the sum total of the soul, with the assistance of spirit guides and other highly evolved beings.

Westerners tend to resist the idea that humans can reincarnate in nonhuman forms, or that nonhuman forms may "graduate" to human bodies. While some persons do claim to regress to nonhuman life forms under hypnosis, they are in a very small minority.

A strong Western belief is that karma is not immutable, but may be mitigated by forgiveness and a change in consciousness, and by the concept of grace. Grace, in Christian terms, is God's mercy offered through Christ, salvation for those who cannot or will not save themselves. There are differences of theological opinion as to whether grace alone is sufficient for salvation, or must be augmented with ethics, work, and the ritual of worship. In mainstream Christianity, grace, of course, applies to salvation in terms of heaven, but reincarnationists apply it to reincarnation.

Grace figures significantly in the readings of Cayce, who characterized it as both a state of mind and a gift from God. Grace comes into play when one contemplates an evil deed and then has a change of heart, realizing that the act is wicked and should not be committed. It comes into play when one forgives others for wrongs. Grace, it is believed, has the power to supersede karma because it engenders a growth in spirit. Otherwise, the lessons of karma may be lost. Grace assumes that God does not wish to punish people for their sins, but to help them learn from their mistakes. In interpreting the Cayce readings, author Lynn Elwell Sparrow, in *Reincarnation: Claiming Your Past, Creating Your Future,* provides an excellent example of karma versus grace. A woman abandons a child to an unknown fate in order to preserve herself. Under the law of karma, she returns as an orphan. Under the law of grace, she returns as a social worker who serves children.

Grace must not be misinterpreted as an "out" for transgressions. To knowingly commit a wrong and then be "sorry" for it is not grace.

In the Age of New Consciousness, reincarnation has come to be seen as a means of transformation. Through an understanding of both karma and grace, one can examine oneself in various roles and situations and learn from them and grow spiritually.

CHAPTER TWO

Spontaneous Recall
of Past Lives

Just before we are reborn, a veil of forgetfulness is said to descend to block our remembrance of our past lives. We come into life with a karmic history and a purpose, yet we have no conscious access to either. According to Eastern doctrine, forgetfulness is a blessing that enables the soul to make a fresh start in each incarnation. Otherwise, life would be extremely complicated and confusing, perhaps even paralyzing. Nonetheless, we glimpse the past at certain moments. Fragments and fleeting impressions and feelings bubble to the surface, only to be passed off as imagination in many instances. In some cases, a person may be swept into an incredible vision that unfolds before his or her eyes.

There are many ways to experience past lives spontaneously, that is, without making a deliberate effort to do so.

Déjà Vu

Déjà vu is an unexpected and unexplained feeling of familiarity in relation to places, events, people, dreams, and all manner of other experiences. A French term for which there is no exact English equivalent, déjà vu generally means "already seen." It is a common experience: you meet someone for the first time, yet feel you have known him before; you visit a strange place for the first time and feel oddly at home. Déjà vu varies in intensity, from a vague feeling of familiarity to specific knowledge, such as how to get around a strange city, or the location of hidden objects in a strange place.

Many scientific theories have been advanced since the late nineteenth century to explain the phenomenon, yet none has been adequate. Perhaps the best explanation is that déjà vu is the surfacing of fragments of past-life memories.

Carl Jung once had a powerful déjà vu experience. During his first trip to Africa, he traveled by train from Mombasa on the the rugged Kenyan coast to Nairobi. Looking out the window at dawn one morning, he saw a steep red cliff on which a lone black man stood, leaning on his spear, watching the train. Jung felt an intense déjà vu. He wrote in his memoir *Memories, Dreams, Reflections*, "I had the feeling that I had already experienced this moment and had always known this world which was separated from me only by distance in time. It was as if I were this moment returning to the land of my youth, and as if I knew that dark-skinned man who had been waiting for me for five thousand years." The curious sensation of familiarity stayed with Jung throughout the rest of his journey through Africa. He called the feeling a "recognition of the immemorially known."

WAKING VISIONS AND INTUITIVE FLASHES

Visions and instances of past lives can arise during waking consciousness, triggered by déjà vu, meeting someone with whom one has a karmic bond, visiting a place tied to a past life, even hearing music or seeing art that has a past-life meaning for the individual.

The visions may flash quickly across the mind's eye or may appear as hallucinations, in which the present surroundings disappear and are replaced by scenes from the past, and the viewer feels transported in the flesh to another time and place. All the senses are engaged, and for a few brief moments the person relives the past. Sometimes the past-life connection is sensed merely as an intuitive "knowing" without conscious reasoning. Such intuition plays an ancillary role in past-life recall, reinforcing what one experiences through other forms mentioned here. Intuitive flashes can provide supplemental details to a recall and give insight into karmic situations.

In his book *Lifetimes: True Accounts of Reincarnation,* Frederick Lenz formulated a model for a waking vision recall, based on his interviews with 127 people. A person is engaged in a normal activity, and becomes aware of a high-pitched ringing or buzzing in one or both ears. The noise grows louder until all other noises are blocked out. He notices that his body feels light. His surroundings begin to change, becoming hazy and wavy as though everything around him is vibrating. Colored lights may pass before his eyes. He feels ecstatic, and strange scenes begin to appear, as though he is watching a movie. At some point, he realizes he is no longer watching the movie but participating in it. His consciousness may switch back and forth between that of viewer and participant. Eventually, the scene fades and he becomes aware of his body once again.

Lesser phenomena associated with waking visions include an awareness of being out-of-body during the experience, and being guided by a voice or angelic being. In a nonjudgmental fashion, this guide presents an overview of the past.

In some cases, individuals see more than one life. The guide presents scenes from many lifetimes, from a few to hundreds. The lives are laid out like a string of beads or pearly globes, or are strung out like a series of photographs. They flash by quickly yet are completely understood by the witness, who feels an amazing capacity to absorb tremendous amounts of "knowing" in some sort of telepathic fashion. It becomes instantly clear what has and has not been learned through a series of lives. While witnesses can see the positive things, more often than not the review serves as a helpful prod to the viewer to reevaluate time that is wasted as the person is mired in hate, jealousy, greed, apathy, or other negative conditions. Often, after such an experience the person is more motivated to seek higher spiritual development.

DREAMS

Some investigators of reincarnation have found that dreams comprise one of the most common sources of past-life recall. Jung was skeptical about reincarnation yet investigated it, looking for empirical ("hard") evidence that would prove the phenomenon existed. He found nothing—déjà vu was not empirical—until he had a series of dreams "which would seem to describe the process of reincarnation in a deceased person of my acquaintance," as he wrote in *Memories*. "But I have never come across any such dreams in other persons, and therefore have no basis for comparison. . . . I must confess, however, that after this experience

I view the problem of reincarnation with somewhat different eyes.''

Past-life dreams may occur once in a great while or with great frequency. Distinguishing past-life dreams from ordinary ones is not always easy. Individuals who have experienced many past-life dreams learn to recognize them by the impressions they create. Such dreams usually are extremely vivid and clear and remain sharp in the memory for a long time. Many are lucid dreams, in which the dreamer is aware that he or she is dreaming, perhaps even knowing the dream is a recollection of a past life. Recurring dreams often have past-life connections. Interpreting them, however, frequently requires the help of a therapist who specializes in past-life recall. To help with later interpretation, dreams should be recorded in a notebook or journal immediately upon awakening.

Past-life information also can surface in the twilight periods at either end of the sleep cycle: the hypnagogic state, which occurs as we drop off to sleep, and the hypnopompic state, which occurs as we rise to wakefulness. In these states, we experience reveries— snatches of images and voices. The reveries usually seem like nonsensical jumbles, but may contain psychic or past-life information that, in these states, is not filtered out by the conscious mind.

SPONTANEOUS MEMORIES

The ability to remember a past life spontaneously, as though it were just another memory from yesterday or last week, is rare, but from a scientist's point of view, quite significant. Spontaneous recall usually occurs in children between the ages of about two and four. By age three, children have learned enough vocabulary skills to describe, even if only in a rough outline, what they remember. By age eight, the past-life memories have begun to fade or are already obliterated by the memories accumulated in the present life.

Scientists view spontaneous recall in children as significant because in many such cases, children talk about and can identify people, places, and things they have no way of knowing. They exhibit knowledge and skills they have not been taught and often demonstrate intimate knowledge of a deceased personality's life. In the eyes of science, these cases constitute the strongest evidence in support of reincarnation, though they do not necessarily prove its existence. In contrast, an adult who experiences spontaneous recall might possibly be drawing subconsciously upon dozens of sources "forgotten" by the conscious mind—old memories of experiences, or books and movies, for example. In addition, scientists hypothesize that extrasensory skills might also come into play with adults, including receiving information through clairvoyance or telepathy.

One of the world's leading researchers of cases of spontaneous recall is Dr. Ian Stevenson, professor of psychiatry at the University of Virginia and director of the division of personality studies at the university's medical center. Stevenson has investigated reincarnation claims since the 1960s, and has collected data on more than 2,000 cases. Not surprisingly, most of these have occurred in Eastern countries where religious beliefs support the idea of reincarnation. In 1986, just 91 cases of spontaneous recall in American children had been reported, but not all were investigated. Stevenson suggests that Western cases are few because parents typically ignore or discourage a child's talk about a previous existence, or attribute it to imagination. To verify a claim, Stevenson undertakes a lengthy and painstaking investigation, visiting the child and his family, the family of the deceased personality (where possible), and others.

Many of Stevenson's cases involve violent death. The children often remember quite well how they died in the previous life, and may have birthmarks coinciding with the site of the death wound, as well as phobias related to the means of death, such as a fear of water due to drowning. The intense emotions and trauma generated by a violent death probably make it easier for such memories to surface. The interval between such a death and reincarnation often is short, in a few cases less than the gestation period of nine months, indicating perhaps that the soul does not necessarily inhabit a fetus from conception. The Eastern belief is that individuals who suffer violent death are granted the opportunity to be reborn quickly, in order to finish out their karma.

THE RESONANCE METHOD

A resonance is a sound that continues in the ear or memory; we say that something is "resonant" if it has a prolonged, subtle, or stimulating effect beyond the initial impact. The same may be said for past lives: they continue to resonate in the present in a multitude of ways both dramatic and subtle.

A means for discovering these echoes, the Resonance Method, was developed by Michael Talbot, a Manhattan author and a believer in reincarnation. In his book *Your Past Lives: A Reincarnation Handbook,* Talbot defines past-life resonances as "an inexplicable tugging at your heartstrings, a special draw that you feel toward some things and not others when there is no logical reason in this life for you to feel the way you do." Resonances occur in natural affinities for places, things, cultures, races, periods in history, foods, hobbies, occupations, styles of music and art, clothing, religions, languages, and climates. Resonances also surface in dreams, daydreams, inspired thoughts, déjà vu, and what Talbot calls an innate "bedrock knowing." They may be discovered in personality traits and relationships with animals and people. Even dislikes and aversions are resonances. In an interview, Talbot explained:

We have enormous contact with our past-life memories, but they are separated from us by a thin film, so we don't know they are memories. They surface in the form of resonances. I think most resonances have past-life echoes to them. You can't take a single resonance and say, "This is a past-life memory," but they do piece together if you keep lists of them. It's like putting together a giant jigsaw puzzle on a table—none of the pieces make any sense until all of them come together in a larger constellation of information. When I started developing the Resonance Method, it was astonishing to me how well it worked.

The Resonance Method was itself a kind of resonance. I think I always knew it. I was thinking about what I felt resonances for, and the question occurred to me, "I wonder if I've ever lived in Berlin?" I immediately had this feeling, *not really*. I was startled that I knew the answer just like that. So I started asking myself questions and realized there were lots of things in me that I had always known.

When you ask yourself questions about resonances, you don't try to answer them intellectually. We are all incredibly psychic. There is a knowing within us that is below all the chatter in our heads, and it will give us answers to questions. Just ask and listen.

One method I use a great deal is I tell myself I am going to remember. The way we process our earth memories is through contact with our unconscious, and one of the most powerful ways we have that contact is through habit. You establish the habit of remembering. . . . Ian Stevenson said that when you investigate [reincarnation] you have to be a lawyer, a historian, and a psychologist. That is what I always recommend to people. You have to be all those three things, and you cannot jump to conclusions.

Talbot recommends recording resonances in past-life journals or on index cards. Jot them down when they occur to you. Ask yourself questions about places, things, and so on, and note down the answers that automatically arise. Besides spontaneous occurrence, resonances may be coaxed into consciousness through divination, psychic readings, hypnosis, guided meditation, and other forms of enhanced recall.

Resonances have helped Talbot discover at least twenty past lives in varying degrees of detail. His own resonances began early in childhood, when he became aware that he possessed memories that were part of other lives. Up until age five, he refused to call his parents "Father" and "Mother," addressing them instead by their first names. He was strongly drawn to the Asian culture, and displayed a fondness for strong black tea and sitting cross-legged on the floor. Before going to bed, he recited the traditional child's prayer, "Now I lay me down to sleep . . ." but added a Buddhist-like ending, asking God "to release the suffering of all conscious beings."

When Talbot was older, he explored fragments of memories and his resonances with the Far East and, with the help of a psychic, discovered he had at least two past lives as a Buddhist monk. One involved death by drowning:

> One of my earliest memories was that of drowning. I remember drowning twice. In one memory, I was out in the open sea and there was a ship involved. In the other, land was in sight where I drowned. In the second memory, I looked up, knowing I was drowning, and saw the surface of the water without being able to reach it. I could see the faces of men looking down at me through the water. They were dark-complected and wore orange robes, and they were bald. As I grew older, I realized they were monks of some kind. I was puzzled. Who were these men? For a while, I thought I had been ritualistically drowned. I was always looking for some account of ritualized drowning in different cultures and never found it. I was angry toward that memory. Why did they let me drown?
>
> When I had my first reading with [psychic] Jim Gordon, I told him I thought I had drowned before. He said I had drowned twice. One time I was on a ship. It didn't seem to be significant, and it didn't have that much emotional or psychological impact for me. The second time did. I was a monk in India. I knew I'd lived in India before and that I'd been very religious, if not a monk, because I have such a strong feeling for Hinduism and Buddhism and for India in general.
>
> In this past life I was a Buddhist monk. There was a storm, a terrible monsoon, and I sought refuge in a Hindu ashram. They would not let me in because I was Buddhist. I kept walking and got lost in the storm. I fell off a precipice into the ocean and drowned. Gordon said I have held a great deal of resentment toward those monks even

in this life, and this is why I held onto the image of them in my mind as I died.

One could make the argument that a psychic is just picking up on your fantasies telepathically. But Gordon took a story that I had in my mind, offered a different interpretation, and made it make more sense. If he was merely telepathic, at the very least it would mean that I myself did not know the whole story. It was something spun by my unconscious mind that he had to bring out for me.

Resonances act as powerful triggers to past-life memories. Past lives that have the greatest resonance with the present life, in terms of emotions, events, and circumstances, are the most likely to be recalled.

ILLNESS AND ACCIDENT

Severe illness, especially involving high fever, delirium, and coma, sometimes triggers past-life recall. Accidents involving severe trauma, especially to the head (as in concussions), also jar loose past-life memories. In 1907, three-year-old Dorothy Eady of London tumbled down a flight of stairs and was pronounced dead by a doctor. An hour later, the child was revived completely and seemed to have suffered no injuries or ill effects from her terrible fall.

However, Eady soon began having strange dreams of a large building with columns and an exotic garden. She cried that she was not "home," but didn't know where "home" was. Then, on a visit to the British Museum, the child was excited by Egyptian artifacts, and declared that she had found her people. By age seven, she had identified the building in her dreams as the temple of Sety the First, pharaoh of Egypt in the Nineteenth Dynasty, who lived from 1306 to 1290 B.C.

As she grew older, Eady pursued an intense study of Egyptian history. Her story is chronicled in the book *The Search for Omm Sety* by Jonathan Cott.

In 1918, she awoke one night to see a face bending over her—the face of the mummy of Sety. The hands and arms of the figure moved, but it said nothing. After that, she began having a recurring dream in which she was a young Egyptian girl who was beaten with a stick for refusing to answer questions. Gradually, she discovered that she and the pharaoh, who was then in his early fifties, had been passionate lovers. She was a fourteen-year-old orphan, Bentreshyt ("Harp-of-Joy"), who served as a priestess of Isis in Sety's temple at Abydos, the building she had seen so often in her dreams. At age twelve, she'd taken vows to remain a virgin and become the property of the temple. She fell in love with Sety, however, and became pregnant by him. The temple high priest tried to beat the truth out of her, but rather than reveal it, she took her own life.

Eady knew instinctively that in order to contact the spirit of Sety, she would have to move to Egypt. At the age of twenty-nine, she married an Egyptian man and went to live in Cairo. She had visions and saw ghosts at many Egyptian ruins, and she worshiped the ancient Egyptian gods. More remarkably, she was able to resume her 3,000-year-old love affair with the spirit of Sety.

At first, she could only feel his presence. Then one night he sent the spirit of an ancient Egyptian priest to fetch her in her astral body. She awoke and, growing very light, followed the priest through a black fog until they arrived at Sety's palace at Amenti. Inside was Sety, who proposed that from then on, he materialize to her in solid form as he had appeared when they were lovers, a vigorous man in his early fifties. She consented, and he thereafter appeared often, making tender and passionate love to her. He told her he intended to marry her at Amenti; apparently, however, it could not happen until she left her life as Dorothy Eady.

Eady, who had become known locally as Omm Sety, desired to return to the temple of Abydos, even though it meant she would once again become "temple property." The opportunity arose in 1956. When she informed her ghostly lover, Sety told her that he would continue to visit her, but that they would never again make love. If they resisted temptation during the rest of her life at the temple, he said, their original crime would be forgiven and they could be together for eternity.

In the village of Arabet Abydos, Eady's opportunity was work at a low-paying job as a draftswoman to help in the restoration of her beloved temple. The strange Western woman who seemed so at home in the antiquities of Egypt mystified the locals, who feared her as a witch or an adept of Egyptian magic. Conditions there were primitive—she lived in a mud-brick hut with no running water, plumbing, or electricity—but she was infinitely happy. Sety visited her and they spent nights in each other's arms, but refrained from making love. Eady rarely spoke of her secret life to anyone, even close friends. She confined her confidences to her diaries.

Eady died on April 21, 1981. She was buried facing west, toward the Land of the Dead, in the desert north of the Sety and Rameses temples. Undoubtedly her freed soul headed straight for the palace at Amenti, for the long-awaited reunion with Sety, her soul mate and lover.

CHAPTER THREE

Induced Recall of Past Lives

Most individuals interested in discovering past lives must rely on various ways to induce the memories or to otherwise obtain past-life information. The most common methods and avenues are described below.

HYPNOSIS

The concept of reincarnation didn't really attract much attention in the West until the 1950s, when a Colorado housewife's recollections under hypnosis of a past life as "Bridey Murphy" in eighteenth-century Ireland were publicized in the press and in the book *The Search for Bridey Murphy* by Morey Bernstein. The case created a maelstrom of controversy, alternately being denounced as a hoax and hailed as proof of life after death.

The case began in 1952 when Bernstein, a business executive and skilled amateur hypnotist in Pueblo, Colorado, tried an experiment to find out if human memory could be regressed to a period before birth.

His subject was twenty-nine-year-old Ruth Simmons (a pseudonym), who, he discovered, had the ability to enter an "uncommonly deep" trance. Under hypnosis, Simmons went back to the life of a little girl in Cork, Ireland, named Bridget (Bridey) Murphy. In regressions over a period of time, Bridey's story emerged. She had lived between 1798 and 1864. She had married a man named Brian MacCarthy and had died at age sixty-six, withering away after falling down some stairs and breaking the bones of her hip. She gave detailed descriptions of her world, and used archaic Irish slang. Despite shrill denunciations and attempts to discredit it, the case remains one of the most convincing on record supporting the concept of reincarnation.

While the Bridey Murphy case brought reincarnation to the attention of the contemporary public, it was by no means the first regression recall. At the turn of the twentieth century, Colonel Albert de Rochas, a French psychic investigator, undertook a systematic study of past-life regressions. A hypnotist in the style of Mesmer (who placed patients in trance by making hand passes in front of the body), Rochas regressed nineteen French men and women beginning in 1904. The subjects regressed easily and gave descriptions of varying degrees of detail. One young Frenchwoman said she had lived before as "Lina," daughter of a fisherman in Brittany, and had thrown herself off a cliff into the sea after her husband had been killed in a shipwreck. In going through the death experience, the subject gasped and writhed as she "drowned." Rochas attempted to verify his cases but met with little success; the information simply couldn't be found or, in some cases, contradicted what had been reported by his subjects.

In the 1960s and 1970s, past-life recall under hypnosis began to gain popularity as a psychotherapy tool.

Psychotherapists discovered that going back to past lives to confront traumas often speeds the patient's healing. Today, hypnosis is the most common means of induced past-life recall. Beginning in the 1970s, hypnotist Dick Sutphen, now of Malibu, California, was among those who brought past-life regression to the general public by way of group seminars around the country.

There are three levels of hypnotic trance. The first is light trance, in which the patient feels very relaxed and probably does not realize he or she is hypnotized. The patient remains aware of what is going on, internally and externally. An estimated 95 to 98 percent of the adult population can be put into this altered state. According to Dr. Bruce Goldberg in *Past Lives, Future Lives,* information obtained from someone in a light trance often is sketchy, but is adequate for working with phobias, habits, anxiety, and depression. Light trance is also known as "guided meditation," "alpha-state meditation," "guided visualization," and "guided imagery," among other terms, all of which seem less intimidating than "hypnosis."

The second level is medium trance, which can be achieved by an estimated 70 percent of the adult population. In this state, the subject may be aware of outside noises but is not distracted by them. Medium trance is considered ideal for most regressions, because the person can relive and feel the experience, and the information is much more detailed.

The third state is deep trance, accessible to only about 5 percent of adults. The subject is not aware of the experience and will remember what transpired only if given the instruction to do so. Some therapists prefer to work at this level. While some individuals have learned how to hypnotize themselves, most still prefer to work with another person. Because hypnosis and past-life regression can stir up potentially troubling material, *it is very important to undertake regression only with a skilled and qualified therapist.*

People usually try hypnotic regression in order to resolve issues and problems in their present lives, like phobias or physical complaints that have resisted medical diagnosis, obesity, problems in relationships, and the feeling of being off-track in career or overall life purpose. Some merely want to explore past lives out of curiosity or to learn more about themselves. Alice T., a past-life regressionist in Manhattan, has a typical clientele comprising predominantly creative and performing arts professionals, physicians, psychiatrists, attorneys, stockbrokers, academics, and others in white-collar occupations. "Information from a regression often brings the root of a problem into focus, acting as a catalyst for the individual to seek out other forms of self-exploration or therapy," she said. The Higher Self and/or spirit guides select the past lives that are most relevant to each situation.

Hypnotic regressions may be done individually, in couples, or in groups. Individuals and couples can set their own agendas and pace, while those in groups cannot. Group regressions usually are theme-oriented, focusing on a period of history, lives as the opposite sex, lives of power, and so on.

A regression begins with physical relaxation. The person lies down or reclines and is led to relax with background music and suggestion. The eyes are closed. To deepen the altered state of consciousness, practitioners usually direct clients to mentally walk down stairs or enter a tunnel where, at the bottom or the end, they are asked to visualize a light. When the client reaches the light, he or she will then step out into a past-life scene. The therapist then "grounds" the person by having him "look" at his feet in his mind and then the rest of his body to describe what he is wearing.

What is encountered in the scene that follows varies greatly according to the individual. "The large majority of people get some sort of visual images," said Alice. "For some, it is like watching a three-dimensional movie, while others see scenes only in still photographs. Some see in color, others only in black and white, and a few see things in silhouette. Some just get a flash or an intuitive impression. Other senses may be involved as well. Some people hear voices, conversations, and music, and can smell, taste, and feel. Emotions may come through. Typically, a person experiences combinations of sensory impressions, which sometimes vary from life to life."

One example of vivid, nonvisual sensations comes from a young American woman who viewed numerous lives in which she was not very intelligent, and one in which she was a primitive man with no language skills. The nonvisual phenomena accompanied the visual images:

I was a wench in England who was knocked up by a soldier. When I got into this past life, I felt my mental capacity close down. Everything I looked at was filtered through the eyes of a very simple, unintelligent woman. I could feel her personality very strongly.

[In another session] I wanted to see my very first life on this planet. I was a caveman. I was hairy but not animallike. I lived in a commune and hunted. I saw myself standing outdoors looking up at the stars. They were amazing because [in this life] I had never seen stars like that—they were bigger and cruder in shape. They didn't seem as far away as they do now. I had a frustrated feeling because I couldn't speak—there wasn't any language. I had thoughts I wanted to communicate, but I couldn't gather them and give them form. As I was looking up at the stars, I was uncomfortable in my body, trying to put into words what I was feeling. It was like being in jail in my own body.

I communicated with the other humans with drawings. Also, we seem to have had a crude sign language that was almost telepathic. We couldn't communicate concepts, only simple things like meals being ready.

Some individuals see or sense their surroundings quickly and clearly, while others have difficulty at first. The therapist keeps the regression moving by asking objective questions and giving directions, such as "go to the next significant scene in this life" or "go to your last moments in this life." Part of a regression involves going through the death that ends a life. During this phase, the viewer is instructed to feel detached from the death and to play the role of observer. Nonetheless, some deaths, especially violent ones, can be extremely traumatic, which is why it is so important to work with a competent therapist.

Overall, good therapists will not plant suggestions or interpret what the viewer is experiencing, but will allow the subject to make his or her own discoveries. The information revealed is presumably chosen by the Higher Self or the guides as what is needed for growth.

Sandee Mac, a Houston hypnotherapist and spiritual counselor, has been regressing clients since the late 1970s. At the end of a regression, Mac invites present and past selves to meet each other and exchange gifts and information. A gift can be a hug, a beam of light, or whatever seems fitting to the individual. The exchange of information enables the lessons and solutions to crystallize for the client, who sees a sort of karmic balance sheet from the past and the effect it has on the present. The positive energies released from such an inner journey carry on into daily life, often inspiring fresh ideas, an expanded sense of self-awareness and understanding, confidence, and renewed energy.

Hypnotic "progressions" may be taken into the future. These tend to be hazier than views of past lives, perhaps because of uncertainty or apprehension on the part of the viewer, or perhaps because the future is ever changing in response to circumstance and free will. Perhaps more than anything, future progressions help foster hope and desire, and when hope and desire take shape, action follows.

PSYCHIC READINGS AND CONSULTATIONS

Access to past-life information may often come with the help of psychics and channelers, some of whom specialize in past lives. Their techniques vary. Some psychics get past-life information about clients through their own dreams, while others use retrocognition, a type of clairvoyance in which one sees into the past. Channels communicate with their clients' Higher Selves or spirit guides to obtain past-life information.

In a psychic reading, past-life information is given to the client without the client undergoing hypnosis. The disadvantage for the client is that he or she does not actually see the images. However, the information may fit with fragments already known to the client, who can then organize pieces into a whole.

Past lives often surface spontaneously in psychic readings, even when the client is not seeking information on them. The reason for the reading may, unbeknownst to the client, involve unresolved issues from the past. Laurie McQuary, a well-known psychic consultant in the Portland, Oregon, area, often forms images of her clients' past lives when she conducts readings. "If I feel the person is open to it, I will pass along the information," she said. "Sometimes it doesn't apply to the reading, so I don't bring it up. I don't ever do a reading that is all devoted to past lives unless I feel that the person can look at them objectively and can benefit from the experience."

Although examining past lives can prove to be beneficial and therapeutic, McQuary advises her clients to do so with prudence: "I like people to balance themselves. I don't like it when they get so involved in the past that they forget the present, or want to blame the past and not live for today. Frankly, there are things you wouldn't want to look at in your past lives. Certainly we're always learning, but we don't need to have *everything* from the past at a conscious level."

In reading for clients, McQuary occasionally gets glimpses of her own past lives as well. She reported one amusing incident: "I have a former associate, whom I met for the first time at a reading. I said, 'You know, we've had a past life together.' She said, 'Yes, I can feel that.' I could see it clearly. We were in Pompeii. I was a cantina dancer, or whatever they called a cantina then. I said, 'You and I never lived for anything but the moment. We were having a glass of wine when they were hollering "Volcano!" and the lava was rolling down and everyone else was running. We said, "Oh, no, we've got time for one more." ' We laughed about that."

MEDITATION AND YOGA

Past-life recall is sometimes a spontaneous by-product of meditation, though meditation can also be used intentionally to induce recall. In meditation, the body is relaxed and the mind is in an altered state of consciousness. In such an altered state, comparable to the hypnagogic/hypnopompic states mentioned in Chapter Two, the mind is much more attuned to information that flows along psychic channels, which is usually blotted out by the noise of conscious thought. It also is more receptive to information floating up from the unconscious, where past-life memories lie buried.

Pantanjali (who lived about 300 or 400 A.D.), the compiler of the Yoga Sutras, or truths, stated that memories of past lives may be awakened by those who master yoga meditation. According to the Sutras, which are still practiced, the memories, including all details of past lives and all impressions of karma, reside in the *chitta,* or subconscious mind. Their recall is considered a ''miraculous power'' of yoga, attained after long study on the part of the yogi, sometimes stretching over lifetimes.

TRANCE AND ENHANCED RECALL

Some people develop their own methods of tuning in to past lives with combinations of altered state, meditation, and psychic and astral projection skills. Edgar Cayce, who became famous for the trances in which he diagnosed illnesses and prescribed cures, found the root of most physical and emotional ailments in past-life karma. Cayce said he got his past-life information from the Akashic Records, which are said to be the master records of every thought, deed, and emotion in the universe since its beginning. The records exist as impressions upon the astral plane; Cayce described them as traveling on waves of light. Those who learn how to access them may view past lives, much like looking up a biography in a library.

While in trance, Cayce would feel himself leave his body and begin moving through a shaft of light. In misty realms beyond the light, he saw other beings who pleaded for his help or tried to wave him aside, but he ignored them. The beings gradually took on more form and began helping him along his way. His destination was a hill, where there was a huge temple. It seemed to be a cosmic library, filled with books on every life since time immemorial. Cayce would find the book on his particular client and look up the answers to the client's questions.

The British novelist Joan Grant called her enhanced recall technique "far memory." After a childhood during which Grant had numerous psychic experiences, she taught herself how to shift her consciousness to her past-life personalities so that she could look out through their eyes and so relive their lives. During her altered states, she dictated what she saw, did, and felt. Grant has published seven of her past lives as novels (see Chapter Thirteen). She believes she first learned far memory in a past life as a priestess and ruler in ancient Egypt.

Grace Cooke, the British Spiritualist who founded the White Eagle Lodge, a Spiritualist organization, was skilled in meditation. An Eastern adept taught her a meditation technique that enabled her to rise through her crown chakra to the astral plane, where she read the Akashic Records. She learned of her past lives as a Mayan priestess, Minesta, and an Egyptian priestess, Ra-min-ati, the stories of whom she recorded in her book *The Illumined Ones.*

She said the Mayan priestess, Minesta, lived about 10,000 years ago in the Andean foothills of South America. Her civilization had been seeded by extraterrestrials who had first established Atlantis. Archaeologists place the Maya only in Central America and not earlier than about 1500 B.C., which did not dissuade Cooke of the reality of Minesta's world. It is not uncommon in past-life recall to encounter information that runs contrary to the history books. Accuracy often is impossible to judge when there are no surviving records. Yet many people, like Cooke, feel an intuitive certainty about their own versions. When remains discovered in Peru in 1965 showed a Central American influence, Cooke took it as evidence supporting her past life there.

Cooke, who died in 1979, said she was aided throughout her life by the spirit of a Native American, White Eagle, a member of the Great White Brotherhood, the Brotherhood of the Cross of Light within the Circle of Light. White Eagle and other Indian spirit guides appeared to her as a child, and took her on journeys to the astral plane. White Eagle directed Cooke in her spiritual work, as he had done in previous lives, having reincarnated as a Mayan, then an Egyptian priest to be her tutor. She also believed he had incarnated as the legendary Hiawatha, though White Eagle never confirmed or denied this. He told her he had lived as White Eagle, a Mohawk chief and head of the League of Six Nations of the Iroquois.

In her incarnation as Grace Cooke, she continued the spiritual work of her earlier lives, this time as a teacher herself, guiding others who sought to be "channels of light."

MIRRORS

Mirrors have been reputed to have magical powers since antiquity. They are believed to reveal the future and to reflect the soul. They also can reveal the past by giving fleeting glimpses of the faces of persons one has been before. The visions of past-life faces may appear unexpectedly. Some individuals see their own past by gazing into a mirror, much as one would gaze into it to divine the future. By looking steadily into a mirror in dim light or candlelight, one's face seems to undergo changes. Is it a trick of the eye? Many believe not.

Craig Junjulas, a psychic consultant who lives in New Rochelle, New York, has used mirrors extensively in exploring his own past lives, as he explained.

I would look into my eyes, and then my entire face would start to change. I'd see flashes of different faces go by very quickly. Then they would slow down until a single face remained for me to look at. The more I practiced it, the more relaxed I became, and the more I learned—the face telepathically told me about itself.

Among the past lives revealed by the mirror were an Oriental man, a Native American medicine man, a Viking warrior, a Neanderthal, an old Essene, a Greek philosopher, a Greek woman, and a pirate. Each past life presented a different aspect of himself.

The first time I saw a female face looking back at me was the Greek woman, and I had a hard time accepting it. In this life, I was raised in a very macho way. Learning that I had lived as a woman shook me up at first, but had a good impact. Immediately afterward, I started becoming softer in my approach to people.

Junjulas said that watching as your face changes in a mirror can be unsettling, and one should look away or stop if the results are disturbing.

ASTROLOGY

According to professional astrologers, one's natal chart, or horoscope, won't tell you that you were a tailor in Ireland in your previous life, but it can reveal the karmic lessons created by past lives.

The tenets of astrology hold that one's life and destiny are influenced by the positions of the planets at the moment of birth. These positions are depicted in a horoscope, which is divided into twelve houses, each governing a different aspect of life. Beginning with the first house, they are: self; finance; communications; home life; romance, children, and creativity; health, work, and service; marriage and partnership; needs; recognition; career; friendship; and the subconscious.

Each house is related to a sign of the Zodiac, which in turn is ruled by a planet, both of which have certain characteristics. Other planets may be placed in various houses, depending on where they are in the heavens at the birth moment. In addition to determining the placement of planets, astrologers also consider aspects, which are the mathematical relationships of one planet to another.

In her book *Astrology and Your Past Lives,* astrologer Jeanne Avery writes that Saturn, the planet of suffering, karmic burdens, and higher consciousness, provides one of the greatest clues to an individual's past: "The placement of Saturn [in a house] indicates the specific area of life in which the most severe lessons are to be learned, the areas of responsibility are the most pronounced, and restrictions are most likely to occur." For example, Saturn placed in the first house, self, indicates deep insecurity coupled with a strong sense of responsibility, resulting in the need to control and a judgmental character. Past-life regression, perhaps through hypnosis or guided meditation, can explain why those innate conditions exist.

BODYWORK

Therapies that involve manipulation of the body's energy fields frequently trigger fragments of past-life recall, on the part of both the patient and the therapist. The physical body is surrounded by an envelope of energy, the aura. At various points (called chakras in yoga, for example), the Universal Life Force permeates the aura and enters the body. In Chinese medicine, the Life Force is believed to run along twelve meridians in the body, which may be accessed at various points. This force is called by many names, such as *prana, ch'i,* and *ki;* it is essential to health. When the Life Force becomes imbalanced in the body, disease results, and when the Life Force ceases, the body dies.

Past-life fragments may but do not always accompany holistic and alternative therapies to restore balance in the Life Force. They are not uncommon in acupuncture and therapies involving touch and energy transfer like polarity, Reiki, Therapeutic Touch, shiatsu, and rolfing. This last is a hard manipulation of deep muscle tissue designed to release psychological blockages, which possibly could be karmic blocks as well.

Shirley MacLaine, who brought the subject of reincarnation home to millions with her accounts of her own past-life discoveries, received special past-life acupuncture treatments given by Chris Griscom, founder of the Light Institute in Galisteo, New Mexico. Griscom had learned an ancient form of acupuncture using gold needles that opens the "windows to the sky," thus accelerating the passage of energy from higher dimensions into the body and releasing past-life energy relevant to the present life. MacLaine, who described her experiences in *Dancing in the Light,* had been told about previous lives by channeled entities, but wanted to experience them herself.

Griscom worked with her own spirit guides and those of her patients to determine where to place the needles. The guides, she told MacLaine, could see the patterns of past-life memories held in the body's cells. By remembering certain past lives associated with the memory patterns, the subject could release traumatic energy, resulting in spiritual growth and enlightenment.

As MacLaine lay on the table with gold needles in her body, she felt her consciousness shift so that she became both participant and observer of her past lives. Images came in the form of motion pictures, accompanied by emotions and tactile sensations. She viewed dozens of lives, some of which flashed by quickly while others, involving greater lessons, were shown in more detail.

MacLaine relived a remarkable life in India, in which she saw herself as a girl named Asana who could commune telepathically with elephants. Her father in that life had once been kind to a bull elephant. Her father died when Asana was an infant, and for some reason her life had been in danger. The bull elephant took her away from her village to live with his herd. She grew up in complete rapport with the giant and gentle creatures. She taught them to dance, and they in turn taught her to live in the moment and to live without judging others.

Then a tragedy occurred, transforming the relationship between the villagers and the elephants. One of the men in the village killed a friend of Asana's in an argument. Picking up on Asana's thoughts, the elephants understood who the killer was, and the males in the herd wanted to seek revenge. Asana communicated with the female elephants, urging them to restrain the males, who agreed not to kill the murderer, but instead demonstrated their wrath by stampeding through the village and encircling his hut. The villagers, understanding that the elephants had the power to destroy them, established a convenant in which they agreed to maintain peace with one another. Disputes were mediated telepathically by the elephants.

Asana's life explained to MacLaine why she felt an inexplicable fascination with and love for elephants. Her New York apartment was decorated with elephant paintings and figurines. From her Higher Self, MacLaine learned that Asana's life was a crucial one in her spiritual development, for she had learned how to communicate on a collective level with animals, while respecting each animal individually.

Her Higher Self told her that the lesson was that humans should never forget their ability to connect with the collective spirit of animals. MacLaine quoted her Higher Self: "Their [the animals'] energy is essential to our future growth. The animals are on the earth for a reason and our disrespect for them has become alarming. They are totally without ego. Animals would teach us if we would listen. Pulsating in their collective consciousness are the lessons of the past."

Griscom and her colleagues at the Light Institute no longer use needles or any other props, instead relying on techniques of esoteric healing designed to clear the emotional body, that portion of the body's energy field, or aura, which Griscom says absorbs anger, guilt, and fear generated in life after life. These accumulations, like layers of grease, clog up the physical body. The release of negativity from the emotional body facilitates healing.

Yet another oft-used bodywork method in past-life recall is the Christos Technique, the origins of which are rather obscure and attributed to different sources. It was popularized in the mid-1970s by author G. M. Glaskin in his book *Windows of the Mind*. Glaskin said he learned the technique from an article in an Australian magazine. The Christos Technique requires three individuals. The subject lies down and relaxes, while one helper massages his feet and ankles and the second helper uses the outer edge of a clenched hand to massage the third-eye area, which is located in the center of the brow. The third eye, the seat of the brow chakra, governs psychic faculties, and stimulating it can activate one's "clear vision" into the past or future. After the massages comes a series of mental exercises in which the subject is guided to imagine himself growing in length and then shrinking. The ultimate goal is to expand the consciousness beyond the body to visit the past. In variations, ointments are used in the massage.

RHYTHMIC ACTIVITIES

Activities that induce an altered state of consciousness, such as chanting, ecstatic dancing, or rhythmic aerobic exercise such as running, can be conducive to past-life recall. Writing in the *Journal of the Association for Past Life Research and Therapy,* Dr. Marshall F. Gilula recounted how chanting a Tibetan mantra while running opened access for him to a past life as a Tibetan monk. For years, he had seen a "tall, head-less-appearing male spirit figure" within his peripheral vision during meditation. In 1983, shortly after he had begun to chant the mantra during his runs, his voice began to change and become more guttural, and suddenly he realized *he* was the figure he had so often seen while meditating. It came to him that he had been a Tibetan monk or scholar. Over several days, the monk's story unfolded during Gilula's runs.

The monk had been viciously tortured, apparently because others feared some ability of his. He was suspended on a rack or wheel while his eyes were torn out, his flesh ripped, and his hands, feet, and genitals mutilated and then cut off. He was then buried alive but exhumed before death. He was again tortured and cut, and finally stuffed into a brine-filled cask, where he drowned.

Gilula connected the drowning to recurring respiratory problems he had experienced. Almost as if in reaction to the recall, he suffered a severe cold. Over a period of time in which he reviewed the recall, Gilula passed a "sticking point" and began to feel the life forces flowing more freely through his body. After a spiritual consultation that included a past-lives reading, he felt improvements in his breathing during meditation, and in his ability to channel a higher energy for healing.

Past lives can be revisited in various combinations of both spontaneous and induced recall. A hypnotic regression, for example, may be augmented with psychic consultations, channeling, and insights from dreams, déjà vu, and intuitive flashes.

The stronger your intuition, the more receptive you may be to past-life memories floating below the surface of your mind. Intuition is a right-brain phenomenon, associated with creativity and inspiration. One way to strengthen intuition is to pay attention to your gut feelings, which tell you when something "feels right" or "feels wrong." Gut feelings often are ignored or rationalized away by a busy left brain.

The stories in the following chapters demonstrate how varied, rich, and stimulating past-life recall can be. In many cases, the experience served as a catalyst for change and sometimes for profound transformation.

CHAPTER FOUR

Patterns in Past Lives

In 1966, Helen Wambach, an American psychologist and clinical psychiatrist, visited a Quaker memorial in Holly, New Jersey, and suddenly found herself in an altered state of consciousness, feeling as if she were in another time and place.

As I entered the small library room, I saw myself going automatically to the shelf of books and taking one down. I seemed to "know" that this had been my book, and as I looked at the pages, a scene came before my inner eye. I was riding on a mule across a stubbled field, and this book was propped up on the saddle in front of me. The sun was hot on my back, and my clothes were scratchy. I could feel the horse moving under me while I sat in the saddle, deeply absorbed in reading the book propped before me. The book I was reading was a report of a minister's experience of the between-life state while he was in a coma. I seemed to know the book's contents before I turned the pages.

—Dr. Helen Wambach,
Reliving Past Lives

The experience took Wambach by surprise, and led her to investigate the idea of reincarnation through hypnotic regression. After ten years and regression sessions with 1,088 subjects, she had amassed considerable data concerning patterns in past-life regressions, which she published in her first book, *Reliving Past Lives*. As she pursued her study, she began to understand some of the odd cases she had encountered as a psychotherapist since 1955—like Peter, a five-year-old black boy who told her about his life as a rookie policeman who smoked. Peter wanted to smoke and could not understand why he was forbidden to do so. The boy's mother, who said he had talked about the policeman from age three, had discouraged him from "making up stories."

Wambach divided her regressions into time periods from 2000 B.C. to the 1900s; not all her subjects, of course, had lives in each period. She would regress her subjects to a particular time period and ask them about their sex, race, social class, clothing and footwear, utensils, and their death experience. Among her more significant findings were:

—Of the past lives she recorded, 49.4 percent were as females and 50.6 percent as men, which matches true biological balance.

—The large majority of lives fell into the lower class in all time periods, from just under 70 percent in 2000 B.C., to a high of nearly 80 percent around A.D. 500, to nearly 70 percent again in the 1900s. Throughout all time periods, upper-class lives constituted fewer than 10 percent. The middle class reached peaks of between 30 and 40 percent around 1000 B.C. and in the 1700s.

—World population figures, extrapolated from the numbers of lives reported in each time period, matched historical population growth.

Wambach also found consistent descriptions of clothing, footwear, and utensils in given time periods. Of her 1,088 subjects, only eleven gave reports that showed "clear discrepancies" from historical record.

In terms of race, Wambach found that, again, the recalls conformed to history. From 2000 B.C. to about A.D. 500, black and Near Eastern (including Egyptian) lives predominated, followed by Asian and Indian. Caucasian lives fell third, except around the time of the birth of Christ, when they surpassed the Asian/Indian but not the black/Near Eastern. Most early white lives were in the Mediterranean area, with some throughout Central Asia. Around A.D. 400, the three racial types were nearly evenly distributed in Wambach's sample; the Caucasian rate rose steadily to a peak of about 69 percent in 1850, then dropped sharply, while the other two groups rose sharply. Wambach confessed to being most perplexed that one-third of the lives reported from 1900 to 1945 were Asian, and others were black.

Overall, her findings, she felt, ruled out the theory that fantasy or genetic memory accounted for past-life recall.

The following is the story of a Caucasian man who regressed to a primitive life as a black man.

THE LEPER DOCTOR

Doug Hobart is a filmmaker who lives near Portland, Oregon. He and his wife, Sue, assistant managing editor for *The Oregonian,* have long shared a belief in reincarnation and an interest in parapsychology and psychic phenomena. When a friend of theirs went through a past-life regression with a psychic, the Hobarts were intrigued and decided to try it, too. It sounded like fun: you lay down, relaxed in a light altered state of consciousness, and watched your past lives unfold.

The regressions were conducted individually. Of all possible past lives Hobart might have fantasized, the one that materialized astonished him. He found himself in the body of a black man, in a primitive setting that appeared to be the Middle East in pre-Christian times. Hobart described his experience:

I met with the psychic [Marsha] in her apartment. It all seemed so ordinary. I sat and watched a football game with her husband while she finished the dishes in the kitchen. After about five minutes, she was done, and then she led me upstairs to a bedroom. I lay down on the bed. She turned on a tape recorder and sat in a chair next to me. She said, "I'm not going to tell you that this is a past life. I want you to ask yourself why your imagination sees these images." I felt very comfortable with that.

Then she started the relaxation process. I became very, very relaxed. She asked me to focus on a black spot on a white screen, and to enlarge that black spot and enter it, like I was coming into a tunnel. I looked down that tunnel and saw a light at the end. Marsha said to imagine large stone steps, and to step down until I could move into the light. As I moved into the light, she said, "Can you see anything around you?" I said, "No, just a white light." She said, "Look down at your feet." When I looked down—and this was extremely vivid—I saw I had thin, black legs. I laughed and said, "My legs are black!"

I could describe in great detail my legs, the type of sandals I was wearing. The hair on my legs was very dark and wiry. The sandals were leather, with thongs wrapped around my feet. Marsha asked me to look around me. It was hazy, I couldn't see that much. Whenever I had trouble seeing things around me, she would have me look back at my feet and then out again. I laughed every time I looked at my feet. I could wiggle the toes. They weren't my feet, but they responded to my movements. That was fun.

As I kept describing a little more detail about my sandals or the hair on my legs—it was really stubbly, coarse hair—I began to notice what the ground looked like, and things started to get clearer. I could describe the stony ground around me, and then the hillside, which had a kind of sage growing on it. The earth was white, light, and dusty. There was sand, but it was not a desert. The hills had a lot of shale and huge granite rocks. I saw a crow sitting in a madrona-like tree with red, peeling bark. The scene grew like a painting in my mind, and once it was complete, I could see anywhere.

There was a trail, and Marsha had me walk along it and describe what I saw. I could smell goats. I never saw them, but I could smell them very distinctly. It was a strange sensation. I wanted to know what direction I was going, but I could not figure out my direction or the time of day. The light never varied.

As I walked along, I came to a wall made of stacked stones. It was higher than my head. Marsha told me to float up and see what was on the other side. I laughed and said, "I can't do that." She said, "Go up on your tiptoes and you'll just float up." I tried it and it worked. I floated up very high, to where I could see the entire village, including the central well with water jugs around it. There were maybe eight or ten square houses, built into the sides of the hills, and all facing the central well. The houses had thatched roofs. The thatching looked more like coarse bundles of sticks, not grass. There was no furniture that I could see; everything was rather primitive. I didn't see any people, although I could hear them. I couldn't tell if they were speaking a foreign language.

After floating down, I went back to walking on the trail. I would be walking along, and suddenly the scene in front of me would be different. A young girl was suddenly running in front of me. She was about six or seven, with long, straight, dark brown hair and almond brown skin. She was wearing the same type of short, brown, coarsely woven sack that I was wearing. She was smiling and laughing and pointing at me, taunting me to chase her in some kind of game. She was saying my name, but I couldn't catch it.

When I saw this little girl, I started to cry. I *loved* her. I still get goose bumps when I think about it, because I loved her so much, but I didn't know what my relationship was to her. I felt this tremendous yearning—it was overwhelming. I was so surprised. Here I was, lying on this bed supposedly "imagining" these things, and the tears were streaming down my face! At the same time, I had this feeling of joy. I wanted to know her name or get more details about her, but for some reason I couldn't, and that frustrated me. She ran on ahead, and I continued walking and never saw her again. I haven't a clue as to who she was. She doesn't seem to be anyone in my present life.

An odd thing was, as I moved along, I got older. I was walking along the trail at what seemed to be the same speed all the time, but suddenly I would be in a different place, and there would be a change in me. I'd started out wearing this burlap sack that came down to just above my knees. As I got older, I noticed I was wearing the same kind of sack, but it came to just below the knees. I became more aware of the heat as I grew older, because my clothes seemed heavier and stickier.

The leather sandals also changed a little. My feet got flatter and there were more striations on the light bottoms. I also became aware that I now carried a bag. It was made of leather and had drawstrings, so that it would close up like a purse. This strap was across my chest and the bag sat against my right hip. It was bulky and uncomfortable.

I found myself in a fairly wide gully, a canyon that looked like high water had gone through it. There were trees and big rocks on either side. I saw two people coming at me, but I had the feeling they were "things," not people. When they saw me, they cowered away. I said, "I don't like this, I want to get away." Marsha said, "You can't get away. There's nothing to be afraid of. You must face this and see what it is." I repeated, "No, I don't like this, I want to get away." She said, "You're relaxed. This is something you should look at."

Then I saw that these people were lepers. They were all wrapped up and covered with grungy burlap. They cowered, and I had to grab them and turn them around. The next thing I realized, I was kneeling next to one of them, grinding herbs in a mortar. I put fresh leaves in with these dried herbs and made a paste, and put the paste on the skin of the lepers. I could see the cracks and the black, dead portions of their skin. I didn't notice what their skin color was—all I saw were the sores.

I must have been a healer. I used the bag to carry the herbs and the little mortar, which looked like a round river rock. I would get fresh green leaves and add them to the dried herbs to make the paste because there wasn't any water.

The next thing I realized was that I was in a leper colony and I had the same black patches on my arms. The first sore appeared on the top of my forearm. I was still grinding herbs and putting the paste on the arms and thighs of people. The lepers lived in caves that were undercuts in these huge slab rocks. It was cooler in these undercuts. There were depressions, all smoothed out, where people had slept. There were cooking utensils, bowls made out of clay. The lepers just wandered around, waiting to die. I had the impression that I had gone there as a stranger to help them, and all of a sudden I was one of them.

I was way in the back in the cool section of one of these undercuts, sitting cross-legged, always covered up. I had a big blanket over my shoulders, and I hurt. Then I felt a weight on my chest. I was lying down on the ground, and there were two or three other lepers around me. I was in pain. There was an oppressive weight over my entire body, and it was difficult to breathe. I just wanted to curl up in a ball. Everything hurt. I knew I was dying. Then I felt this tremendous weight taken off me, and I floated up. It was total release. This terrible unpleasantness lifted away, and I felt like I was floating up in the sky toward a light. It was wonderful. I didn't even attempt to look back.

Then Marsha started calling to me to feel my feet: "You have to feel your feet. You're here.

Feel your body." She touched my foot. I just lay there. I wanted to continue this floating sensation. The last thing I wanted was to feel my feet. She said, "Are you all right?" I said, "Yeah." She said, "I'm going to go downstairs. You lie here as long as you want." I lay there and went over and over and over everything for a long time.

At first, I didn't feel comfortable talking to anybody about it. I told Sue a little tiny bit that day, but no details. For a long time, every time I thought about that little girl, I started to cry. It took weeks before I could tell my close friends that I'd done this [the regression]. Even then, when I talked to Sue or my parents about it, I still cried. The experience was extremely personal, and I didn't want to share it, because I didn't think anyone could understand how intensely personal it was. People have a tendency to talk about it like a joke. I can joke about it now, but in truth, I take it very seriously. It's still incredibly personal and emotional.

Asked what seeing this past life had meant to Hobart in terms of his present life, he responded:

It reinforced my belief that this life isn't all there is, and that death is just a transition. My attitude toward my life now is much different. I'm able to put the good—and the bad—that happens into a larger perspective. I don't feel devastated by setbacks. I've been through them before and I'm sure I'll go through them again.

SEX CHANGE

Individuals who go through past-life regression often are surprised to find themselves changing sex.

Some men (though not all) have a much more difficult time accepting female lives than women do male lives—a sad reflection of the pervasive male view of women as second-rate citizens. In fact, in some cultures that believe in reincarnation, such as the Druse of Lebanon, men refuse to believe that it is possible to reincarnate as women; it is simply unacceptable. In other cultures, as in Burma, it is sometimes considered punishment for a man to be reborn as a woman.

Ian Stevenson considers the incidence of sex change the most important variation in features of reincarnation cases in different cultures. His research shows that the incidence of reported sex change in past lives does seem to be influenced by cultural attitudes. Stevenson has found no reported case of a male being reborn as a female in Lebanon or Turkey, or among the Tlingit Indians of southeastern Alaska or the Haida, Tsimsyan, and Gitskan Indians of British Columbia. Among cultures that do have reported past-life sex change cases, women remember past lives as men three times as often as men remember lives as women.

The incidence of sex change ranges from a low of 3 percent of reported cases in India to a high of 50 percent among the Kutchin (Athabaskan) Indians of the Canadian Northwest Territories (the Kutchin figure is not Stevenson's finding). Sex change accounts for 12 percent of reported cases in Sri Lanka, 13 percent in Thailand, 15 percent of nontribal U.S. cases, 18 percent in Nigeria, and 33 percent in Burma.

If a man believes that it is either highly undesirable or impossible to be reborn as a woman, does this mean that he doesn't reincarnate as a woman, or that he merely suppresses the memory of female lives? Stevenson has theorized that both answers may be correct. It is certainly likely that undesirable memories will be repressed in order to conform with culture. In addition, Stevenson said, reincarnational beliefs governing sex change might be strong enough to act like "posthypnotic" suggestions after death, thus making reincarnation as the opposite sex less likely.

CAYCE'S SOUL GROUPS

According to Edgar Cayce, souls have reincarnated throughout history more or less in groups in accordance with their alignments to religions, races, cultures, nations, and so on. The largest group comprises the planet's entire population, for earth is not the only place in the cosmos to live, according to Cayce and others. Soul groups are fluid, their ranks constantly shifting as individual souls change course. Generally, however, the groups come and go in earth history in cycles. In the thousands of Cayce readings, two major soul groups were identified: Group One includes souls who lived in early Atlantis, early ancient Egypt, Persia during the time of Croesus I and Croesus II, Palestine, during the Crusades, and in colonial America. Group Two includes souls who lived in late Atlantis, late ancient Egypt, early Greece, Rome during the time of Christ, France during the time of Louis XIV, XV, and XVI, and America during the Civil War.

The souls who lived during any of these times also most likely had other lives. It might be because these were periods of great importance in the course of human events and evolution. In their reincarnations, soul groups are subject to karma and planetary influences. A particular group may not desire to collectively reincarnate, for example, but may be required to do so for the purposes of balancing karma. Some members of soul groups may be present in a particular cycle in spirit form as guides, rather than in the flesh, still wielding an influence upon earthly affairs.

EMERGING SOUL GROUPS

Cayce died on January 3, 1945, shortly before the end of World War II, another great period of world trauma and change. As linear time continues, other watershed periods will undoubtedly mark new soul groups, subgroups, or cycles of groups. Three such groups are emerging:

> World War II casualties
> Vietnam War protestors and casualties
> Native Americans

World War II Casualties

Cases of the reincarnation of the souls of those who died during World War II have been reported; Cayce expressed concern for children killed in the war who reincarnated too quickly and made poor choices for families. The soul group of World War II is complex, for woven through it is the ethnic karma of the Jews, which has extended over 3,800 years of history.

Rabbi Yonassan Gershom of Minneapolis has conducted an informal study that has yielded interesting information about Jews who died in World War II. Writing in *Venture Inward,* the magazine of the Association for Research and Enlightenment, Gershom said the majority of reincarnated Holocaust victims in his survey were born between 1946 and 1953. Most of them were not reincarnated as Jews; those who were typically are marginal in their faith, perhaps, Gershom suggests, because World War II marked their first experiences as Jews. About two-thirds have light hair and blue or hazel eyes. Experiences reported to him include feelings of familiarity and affinity with the Jewish faith, practice of religious rituals and traditions not generally known outside the Jewish community, familiarity with the Hebrew language, and déjà vu or strange experiences upon visiting the sites of concentration camps. One woman who visited a camp felt as though she were walking through mud, even though the paths had been covered with gravel since the war. She recognized the building where she knew she had died, and saw her death. At the end of the tour, her feet and socks were muddy, though her shoes were dry.

Others have reported terrifying nightmares of being killed, as well as phobias of policemen, barbed wire, doctors, and uniforms. Two persons reported asthma attacks brought on by Jewish rituals, attacks reminiscent, Gershom said, of choking to death in a gas chamber.

Some Hasidim believe that Hitler was a reincarnation of Amalek, grandson of the evil Esau, who in the Bible came to represent those who prey on the weak. Exodus 17:16 says that "YH'VH [Yahweh] will be at war with Amalek throughout the ages." This may be taken as a literal reference to the reincarnation of Amalek, or, as Gershom prefers, an indication that God will always fight the oppressor.

Gershom said the Holocaust served as a warning that human rights were in danger, and it has entered the collective unconscious as an archetype of "eternal warning about the misuse of our technology."

Vietnam War Protestors and Casualties

The Vietnam War divided America into bitter factions, and left shattered veterans and broken families to contemplate the horrors of killing. Unlike World Wars I and II, there were no black-and-white issues to define which side was "right" and why. A popular Age of New Consciousness theory holds that the protestors of the Vietnam War were the reincarnated dead of World Wars I and II, who came back angry about the senselessness of war. As the dead of Vietnam return, they, too, are likely to be regretful, angry, or outraged over war. The next chapter presents the story of Bill, who in his previous life died as a soldier in Vietnam in 1965.

Native Americans

The Native Americans were made strangers in their own land by the founders and pioneers of this nation. Their way of life was termed savage and held in contempt by the more "civilized" folk, who proceeded to pollute and destroy the environment. The Age of New Consciousness has rediscovered the Native Americans' ideas about life, spirit, healing, and living in harmony with nature.

If cultural attitudes have the power to suppress certain past-life memories, as with sex change, they also have the power to release them. Therefore, it is not surprising, in light of the interest in Native American culture, that the reported incidence of Native American past lives should be on the increase. In addition, some Native American souls may have reincarnated in the race of their oppressors as a teaching tool, to help bring individuals back into touch with Native American culture and to stimulate interests that are then pursued long after the regression. (Chapters Fifteen, Sixteen, and Seventeen present stories in which Native American past lives figure prominently.)

SUTPHEN'S 25,000

Teotihuacán, in central Mexico, is the site of the ruins of a once splendid ancient city. A religious, cultural, economic, and political center, its population may have reached a peak of 200,000. It was twelve square miles in size, larger than the area contained within the walls of Imperial Rome under the Caesars, a contemporary civilization. By the time the Aztecs arrived in A.D. 1325, it was long deserted and in ruins. The Aztecs named the place Teotihuacán, which means "the place where men become gods."

In 1974, Dick Sutphen and his wife, Tara, visited Teotihuacán and walked among the ruins, including the Street of the Dead, lined with mounds in which the Aztecs believed the gods were buried. Sutphen felt a sense of déjà vu. He experienced a dream in which he was in ancient Teotihuacán. Thousands of people filled the street and the surrounding night. Elegantly robed men lined the steps of the Pyramid of the Moon, atop which was lit a huge fire. In the dream, he was instructed to "get the books together." He didn't have the foggiest idea what that meant.

Through a channeler friend, he found out that he was part of a group of people who had lived at the same time in Teotihuacán, and who had made a pact to reincarnate every 700 years to present the spiritual knowledge that they had possessed at that time. Sutphen was fulfilling that past-life pledge by writing books.

Later in 1974, Sutphen had a psychic vision that was to repeat itself over the years. He was a man dressed in a white tunic with gold braid ribbing, holding a crystal rod and standing on top of the Pyramid of the Sun with fifteen to twenty others. Thousands of people filled the Street of the Dead. He was projecting his will through the rod, which glowed blue-white, to control the masses of people trying to climb the pyramid.

In 1987, Sutphen was awakened in the middle of the night by an inner voice that instructed him it was time for important communications. The voice told him he was one of 25,000 people who had lived 1,400 years ago in Teotihuacán, and he was to assist others of this group who had reincarnated to awaken to this awareness.

According to information revealed in regressions and psychic consultations, the pact had been made in A.D. 581 during a time of political upheaval. Sutphen and his wife, Tara, were part of a secret religious group of sixteen, who were also publicly part of a larger religious council. In a change of political power, the new rulers, a hierarchy of priests, misused their powers and blamed the results on the inner circle, which then disguised its teachings by painting over murals on the walls of the Pyramid of the Sun. The inner circle was finally forced into hiding.

In an effort to make a last, public stand, the group summoned the civilization's population to the Pyramid of the Sun to hear an announcement. About one of every eight people—25,000 in all—appeared, and took the pledge to return every 700 years together. The meeting was scuttled when soldiers arrived and arrested the members of the inner circle and other protesters. The scapegoats were buried alive in pits.

Historically, Teotihuacán began to decline after the late sixth century, and was eventually sacked and partially destroyed.

Sutphen proceeded to search for the 25,000 in his regression seminars. According to their mission, the 25,000 are to once again spread enlightened ideas around the world, so that the fate that befell Teotihuacán will not happen again.

Proving Past Lives

Most people who see their past lives, especially during a light hypnotic trance, wonder if they are "real" or products of their imaginations, even if they "feel true." There is often little to prove the existence of a past life. As seen in Wambach's findings, most past lives are those of ordinary people, for whom few, if any, records exist. Through research one can substantiate historical details of a period, but seldom can one find proof that a certain individual lived. Few regressions provide full names, let alone sufficient biographical information to track down an identity.

In the area of research on spontaneous recall among children, numerous solved cases in which a child names his previous personality, identifies his former family members, and discloses personal information known only to the dead person or his immediate family and friends, would appear to be proof of reincarnation. Scientists, including Stevenson, take a more cautious view: such cases are "evidence in support of reincarnation."

For the typical hypnotic regression, one must rely largely upon intuition in judging reincarnational memories. Most people feel that if they were to fabricate a past life about themselves, they would have conjured up a life of glamour, not the usual mundane existence they encounter. It is common for individuals to receive additional past-life information intuitively, long after a regression session.

Alice T. of Manhattan, who has uncovered more than thirty of her own past lives, observed, "I believe that we have nonphysical beings around us who care about our spiritual development. In a session, I try to strengthen the communication between the client and his or her guides. Sometimes these beings appear in the regression in human or spirit form, or as lights or colors. They help provide answers. Past-life information is surprisingly accessible."

Sandee Mac of Houston believes people do tap into real memories, but she leaves the ultimate conclusion up to her clients. "I suggest that they trust what comes into their minds, but not get caught up in whether or not they are seeing a 'real' past life. The important thing is that they are being given information they need in order to work through something in their present lives.''

Psychics also are asked by clients how to judge the information given them. ''Why can't you just trust your feelings?'' said Laurie McQuary, of Portland, Oregon. ''With imagination, you have thousands of scenarios to choose from. When one strong feeling comes through, if you really explore it, you're going to see it exactly the way it was and not how you wish it had been. Before you start rationalizing whether it's imagination or not, you've got to decide whether you believe in reincarnation. If you do, you don't think about it being imagination. You trust that it's the truth.''

CHAPTER FIVE

Slain in the Vietnam and Civil Wars

Bill (not his real name) is a college student in New England. A native of California born in 1968, he has since early childhood been fascinated by war and the military, and also has felt an affinity with the name "John." It was neither his first nor middle name, yet as a child he adopted it as a second middle name and called himself by it.

His family moved around the country while he was growing up, and in Texas, where he finished high school, Bill met a friend who introduced him to reincarnation, metaphysics, and other topics of the New Age. Just before he entered college, Bill decided to undergo hypnotic regression as an exploration of himself. The night before, he and his friend meditated together to prepare for it.

Three key, related lives appeared in the regression the next day, two of which involved deaths in wars: the American Civil War and the Vietnam War, one soul group and one emerging soul group. The entire experience was intense and emotional, as Bill relived what he encountered rather than merely observing it.

At the start of the regression, Bill told the hypnotist that he wanted to discover information relating to the back problems he had suffered for quite some time. What he saw was a Civil War battle.

I found myself wearing an officer's uniform and leading troops in a hill entrenchment alongside what appeared to be a river. The regressionist asked me to look at the aftermath of the battle from a detached point of view. I saw the hill littered with bodies, and found myself still alive and struggling on my back—evidently I had been wounded in the fighting, which had left most, if not all, of my men dead.

The regressionist asked me to remove the officer from the battle scene to a place where he would be warm and comfortable, and to tell him that I was from the future. She told me to thank the officer for that life and for all that he had learned and done during it. In addition, I should tell him that the injury was in the past and he could let go of it, so that I could be freed from it in the future. The two of us had something to discuss, she said, and would come to an understanding.

I said I sensed there was a bayonet in the officer's stomach. She told me to remove it and take the officer away from the battle scene. "There is something else that Bill in the future needs to know," she said. "What is it?"

After a few moments, I yelled out, "What a waste! My men!" and I broke into tears. The regressionist reminded me to take the officer away from the scene and tell him that the incident was in the past and that I was going to set him free, that I had come back to earth and so had all the [men under his command who had died] who were being given different lives with different options. "Thank him for what he went through," she said. I still felt very anxious. She said, "There is something else, isn't there?"

I screamed, "I was abandoned! They left me!" I went on to say that I had never forgiven myself. The regressionist asked me to forgive myself now, but I cried out that I could not. She then took me to a deeper level to find out why this was so.

I then saw I was in the Arctic Northwest and was a logger or hunter. I got caught out in the cold when my dogsled overturned. I seemed to have broken some ribs and injured myself internally, because I was spitting up blood and couldn't go anywhere. It was very cold. Once I had eaten all my food, I ended up eating my dogs. It was a very cruel and painful thing, and all kinds of emotions popped out that I never realized I had. I was responsible for and loved those dogs, and yet they had allowed me to eat them. I was raging about how faithful they were, because they had a chance to get away. They didn't have to stay with me, but they did, and they gave themselves to me freely. I was overwhelmed. The connection to the war scene made me feel very cruel, and I could not see how I could ever forgive myself.

The regressionist said I did not need to go through that experience anymore, that I could rescue the man and his dogs. She said the man no longer needed to be angry or blame himself. I wanted to know why he had done what he did. I felt very confused. She asked me if I now understood about the Civil War experience and being abandoned, and about forgiving. I said that I did, that I knew I had to forgive myself. I let out one final, biting emotion, crying out, "They were all so young!"

"Forgive yourself for setting yourself up and forgive the men for doing what they had to do," the regressionist said. I did that. Then she told me, "See him fill with light, strong and whole and healthy, and tell him that you are going to release him and watch him go up into the light." I did, and I felt that I experienced a very definite healing.

After the regression, I asked my friend if he had sensed anything when we'd meditated the night before. He said, "You know, I could hear the sounds of dogs and I could taste raw flesh in my mouth." That was quite a shock. I then told him about the man in the woods.

The experience was so powerful that Bill decided to undergo more regressions to learn what lay in his past. In a subsequent session, his regressionist asked if there was another life related to the Civil War life. Bill, who was a small child when the United States finally pulled out of Vietnam, suddenly found himself in Vietnamese jungles, an officer or a noncom leading a small group of about ten soldiers.

We were dropped off by a boat onto a bank. We wanted to go to some village to set up a school or orphanage for children. I don't think there were any orders for it; it was something I thought was important. We got nailed. We didn't get very far into the jungle before we were attacked. My adrenaline shot up. The next thing I knew, I think all my men were killed, and I was lying on my back in pools of blood. It was shocking. I felt everything from fear to hatred to regret. At one point, I blurted out, "I goofed. We didn't need to do this!" It was the same feeling of uncommon duty toward my men that I experienced in the Civil War life.

In the end I just drifted off. Later I had an eerie feeling that I may have survived for some time, maybe I was rescued and they got me onto a helicopter and tried to stitch me up, and I didn't make it.

While he was hypnotized, Bill was able to read his dog-tag number. He thought his name was either John or Tom. Intrigued, he delved into that life in additional regressions in order to recover more details. He decided to try to verify whether or not the man he saw in Vietnam had actually lived. In one regression, Bill discovered the soldier's Social Security number. In his investigation afterward, he discovered that there was in fact a soldier who had that number and who was killed in Vietnam in 1965. The man's name was John X and his name appears on the Vietnam War Memorial in Washington, D.C. Bill was uncertain whether or not he would contact the man's family; such a situation might be like an emotional bomb to them.

Bill also discovered that about five members of his Vietnam detail had reincarnated and were among his friends in high school in Texas.

I think in many respects, the purpose of my being here [in the present life] was to come back and check up on them and make sure they were all right.

I had a dream one night that I was back in our old house. I was very young and was being chased by a spirit. It wasn't evil. The gist was that I had done what I had come to do—check up on these guys—and having fulfilled my end of the bargain, it was time for me to "go home." In the dream I said, "No, I want to stay." I was having a tantrum. I did not want to leave. I said, "There are things to be done here, I'm excited by the challenge."

That's the way I feel. Life is exciting. So I stayed.

Bill did not discuss his revelations with his friends, feeling that he should not push the matter with others who might not be ready for it.

Months after his first regression, he came across information that shed light on his Civil War recall. It seemed like coincidence, but Bill was certain it was synchronicity.

I was flipping through a *Yankee* magazine and found a story about a colonel in the U.S. Army during the Civil War who was in charge of a Negro regiment from Massachusetts. They led an attack on an entrenched beach facility in North or South Carolina in about 1862 or '63. Most of the men in the regiment were killed, including the colonel. This made sense with what I had seen. The colonel was buried in a mass grave with his Negro troops. Evidently his body was desecrated by the Southern soldiers because he had led blacks. In the official Southern account, the colonel was found lying dead next to his color sergeant. Evidently these two had managed to hold out for a while before they were overwhelmed.

The colonel was the son of a very wealthy Northern man. At the end of the war, the army approached the father and said they had located the mass grave where his son was believed to be buried and offered to try to find his body and bury him properly. The father said no, because he felt that his son would have felt honored to be buried with the men he led. Abraham Lincoln said at the end of the war that the one thing that gave the ultimate edge to the North was the Negro soldier, because of his numbers, his courage, and his fighting spirit. I think there is a lot of credibility to that.

I have always had a tremendous respect for blacks and have felt an affinity with them. I think it comes from the respect that I learned for them then.

Bill said that although he could see that in the past he had enjoyed making war—and still felt a fascination with war—he was dismayed by the growth of the war machine in the modern world.

We have pushed our war-making capacity to the limit. There is no need for armies that are so big, missiles that are so powerful. There is no need to turn to genocide and wholesale slaughter to solve political differences.

I had a rare opportunity to look at the "third" side of the story that is so rarely observed, which is the side of the people who get swept up in the events of history: the individual soldier and civilian. As the saying goes, there are those who make things happen and those who watch things happen, and then there are those who wonder what happened. As things unfold in this next century, it's important that we all have an understanding of the significance of the New Age.

If I got anything out of this, it was a unique exposure to the human spirit. So long as it remains strong, so will we.

CHAPTER SIX

The New Atlanteans

Many persons who have undergone past-life regressions during the last two decades have turned up lives in Atlantis. As we saw in the previous chapter, Edgar Cayce identified people of early Atlantis and late Atlantis as parts of two soul groups. He further said that a great influx of Atlanteans reincarnated between the years of 1909 and 1913. Such individuals, especially those born in 1910 and 1911, promised to wield unusual powers for effecting change and influencing world affairs for either good or bad. The original Atlanteans supposedly turned the great powers of their advanced society to serve evil and thus brought about their own destruction.

Most of the individuals seeking regressions in the 1970s and 1980s have been much younger, however, born predominantly from the 1940s through the 1960s. This suggests a new cycle of Atlantean incarnations. Why are so many seeing past lives in Atlantis?

There are several reasons. First, there has been a new surge of interest in ancient cultures, especially in the legendary Atlantis, during the Age of New Consciousness. Second, and more significant, is that many Atlantean recalls deal with *healing*. The Atlanteans are believed to have possessed unusual and remarkably effective healing techniques employing crystals, vibration, sound and music, color, and energy transfer. The Age of New Consciousness has witnessed renewed interest in alternative and holistic healing techniques using the very same tools. Accessing these Atlantean healing lives has in many cases awakened individuals to their own potential healing abilities, as we saw in Chapter One with Pamela Glasser. (Another Atlantean healing story appears later in this book.) Third, Atlantis is a mirror of our own culture: a high-tech, materialistic, and increasingly corrupt and violent society headed down the path of self-destruction. It is possible that Atlanteans have reincarnated in the present in order to help prevent the same fate that befell their own land.

But many people do not believe in Atlantis and say the legend is pure fantasy, highly romanticized by film and fiction. What do we *really* know about Atlantis?

THE ATLANTEAN LEGEND

According to legend, Atlantis was an island continent with a civilization highly advanced in science and technology; these advances were made possible with help from space beings. The Atlanteans' greed, materialism, and corruption eventually led to their downfall, and to the destruction of their entire continent by massive tidal waves, floods, and earthquakes, which sank the land beneath the sea. Some Atlanteans survived, dispersing to other lands around the world, taking their culture and knowledge with them.

No one has ever found any proof that Atlantis existed, yet the legend has remained a powerful one over the centuries. More than forty-five locations on both sides of the Atlantic have been suggested as the site of the great continent.

Plato was the first person known to record the legend of Atlantis, in 350 B.C. in his *Timaeus* and *Critias* of the *Dialogues*. According to Plato, the Greek statesman Solon heard the story of Atlantis from an Egyptian priest. Solon repeated it to Critias, an old Athenian man, who told it to Socrates. The story (told from the viewpoint of the Egyptian priest) takes place in 9600 B.C.

Many great and wonderful deeds are recorded of your State [Athens] in our [Egypt's] histories; but one of them exceeds all the rest in greatness and valor; for these histories tell of a mighty power which was aggressing wantonly against the whole of Europe and Asia, and to which your city put an end. The power came forth out of the Atlantic Ocean, for in those days the Atlantic was navigable; and there was an island situated in front of the straits which you call the Columns [Pillars] of Heracles: the island was larger than Libya and Asia put together, and was the way to other islands, and from the islands you might pass through the whole of the opposite continent which surrounded the true ocean; for this sea which is within the Straits of Heracles is only a harbor, having a narrow entrance, but that other is a real sea, and the surrounding land may be most truly called a continent.

Now, in the island of Atlantis there was a great and wonderful empire, which had rule over the whole island and several others, as well as over parts of the continent: and, besides these, they subjected the parts of Libya within the Columns of Heracles as far as Egypt, and of Europe as far as Tyrrhenia. The vast power thus gathered into one, endeavored to subdue at one blow our country and yours, and the whole of the land which was within the straits; and then, Solon, your country shone forth, in the excellence of her virtue and strength, among all mankind; for she was the first in courage and military skill, and was the leader of the Hellenes. And when the rest fell off from her, being compelled to stand alone, after having undergone the extremity of danger, she defeated and triumphed over the invaders, and preserved from slavery those who were not yet subjected, and freely liberated all the others who dealt within the limits of Heracles. But afterward there occurred violent earthquakes and floods, and in a single day and night of rain all your warlike men in a body sank into the earth, and the island of Atlantis in like manner disappeared, and was sunk beneath the sea. And that is the reason why the sea in those parts is impassable and impenetrable, because there is such a quantity of shallow mud in the water; and this was caused by the subsidence of the island.

—Plato, *Timaeus*

Aristotle, Plato's own student, didn't believe the story of Atlantis and tried to debunk it, saying it was a fiction. So did Pliny and Strabo several centuries later. The story survived, however, and in the Middle Ages, Atlantis was believed to have existed.

Some modern scholars agree with Aristotle and other ancient critics that Atlantis was entirely a figment of Plato's imagination. Nonetheless, the story bears striking similarities to legends in other cultures, including one from the Middle Kingdom of Egypt (about 2000-1786 B.C.) and another in the *Mahabharata* of India. In addition, legends of the native tribes of North, Meso, and South America speak of space gods and races of highly evolved beings. Finally, the flood of Atlantis is perhaps related to the legends of a Great Flood that are found in cultures almost all over the world, with the exception of most of Africa and much of Asia.

In the late nineteenth century, "Atlantology," the study of Atlantis lore, flowered with the publication of *Atlantis: The Antediluvian World,* by Ignatius Donnelly, a U.S. Congressman. Donnelly suggested that the existence of Atlantis could explain unusual similarities between widely separated cultures, such as those of ancient Egypt and the tribes of Central and South America. From his research, Donnelly concluded that:

—Atlanteans comprised at least two races, a small and dark-brown/red-skinned race similar to Egyptians, Berbers, and Central Americans, and a taller white race similar to the Greeks, Goths, Celts, and Scandinavians.

—Atlanteans believed in reincarnation and embalmed their dead.

—There was an established order of priests who oversaw a simple religion.

—The continent itself had 1,500-foot-high volcanic mountains whose tops were snow-covered, elevated tablelands where the royalty lived, a lower "great plain," four rivers flowing from a central point to the four points of the compass, tropical and temperate zones, and fertile soil.

Theosophists, led by Helena Blavatsky, also disseminated views about the long-lost land in the late nineteenth and early twentieth centuries. Blavatsky believed the continent had perished from natural old age, not the corruption of its inhabitants. She said it was formed by parts of Lemuria, which had been destroyed before it. The Atlanteans, who were descended from Lemurians, were giants of twenty-seven feet in height and possessed great psychic powers, she said. They formed the Fourth Root Race of all humans. The priests of the Druids were descendants of the last Atlanteans.

A different picture was provided by one of Blavatsky's followers, Rudolph Steiner, who said he had accessed the Akashic Records to learn about Atlantis. The Atlanteans were weak in logic, he said, but could control life forces and extract energy from plants. Their vehicles hovered a few feet off the ground. They did not possess telepathy, but communicated verbally.

More recently, author Ruth Montgomery, receiving her information from spirit guides through automatic writing, said that the Atlanteans used a Great Crystal for power, and had destroyed themselves by misusing it.

Yet another theory suggests that powerful ley lines converged at Atlantis, which provided its great energy source. Ley lines are lines of natural earth energy said to crisscross the world; where they intersect, they create powerful force fields. Many sacred sites are believed to be constructed at ley-line junctions. Scientists dispute the existence of ley lines, but dowsers say they may be detected and mapped.

Taylor Caldwell's Atlantis

In 1913, at the tender age of twelve, Janet Taylor Caldwell, who later became famous as novelist Taylor Caldwell, wrote a novel about Atlantis. It flowed as if from memory, extraordinarily profound in maturity and sophistication for her age. Later in life, Caldwell said she seemed to "know" about Atlantis from infancy, and was "haunted" by it for years before she sat down to write about it.

The manuscript remained unpublished for about sixty years; by then, Caldwell had undergone hypnotic regression and had discovered that Atlantis figured among her past lives (see Chapter Twelve). Caldwell's Atlantis was a high-tech land of urban overcrowding, rising pollution, power shortages, loss of faith in religion, and social and political upheaval, as well as a haven for immigrants from more oppressed lands. It was ruled by a monarch, who was among the small elite privileged to prolong their lives (to about 200 years) by exposure to rejuvenating chambers and wearing crystals. The continent was divided into twelve provinces, each of which had some autonomy. There were snow-capped volcanoes, great agricultural plains, and a shimmering sea mined for its minerals. The capital city of Lamora was filled with great pillars, domes, and walls of gleaming stone.

In Caldwell's novel, the empress of Atlantis, Salustra, faces the aggression of the neighboring nation, Althrustri. She falls in love with Althrustri's emperor, Signar. Both lands are destroyed by earthquakes and tidal waves; only a handful of inhabitants and the two leaders manage to escape to a new land.

After the novel was published in 1975 as *The Romance of Atlantis* (with Jess Stearn), Caldwell experienced three vivid, exceptionally intense, "big" dreams about Atlantis, in which she was Salustra. The dreams left her weeping for Atlantis and yearning for Signar, whom she knew in her present life but whose identity she never revealed.

Atlantis According to Cayce

Of the 1,600 people who received life readings[1] by

---

[1] Life readings were given to Cayce's family and friends, and concerned previous incarnations that were influencing the present life. The readings were overviews of characteristics, problems, and assets; they are distinguished from the more than 25,000 physical readings Cayce gave to others.

Edgar Cayce, 700 were told they had one or more lives in Atlantis, or Poseidia, as he also called part of it. Cayce said Atlantis was one of the first places on earth where man appeared in material form, as long as 10.5 million years ago. Humans took form and "hardened" by gratifying their material desires. The "red race" had developed Atlantis rapidly, especially in science, technology, and transportation.

The Atlanteans, Cayce said, learned how to amplify the sun's rays with crystals to generate energy for light, heat, transportation, and communication. They wielded "death rays" (perhaps lasers) and enslaved others. Musicians in the temples produced "sounds of all nature" on their instruments. The continent suffered three cataclysms, the third of which destroyed it. The readings give no date for the first cataclysm; the second was said to have occurred around 28,000 B.C. After the first two disasters, many Atlanteans left the continent and migrated to other lands. Others remained behind to rebuild, though a great deal of dissent and discord spread throughout the land. The final destruction apparently was the one cited by Plato, occurring around 9600 B.C. Of Cayce's Atlantean readings, most dealt with the continent's final phase, when the civilization was in decline and suffering great turmoil. The people faced a choice between following God or indulging themselves; too many chose the latter and the culture withered spiritually.

Cayce said the ruins of Atlantis lie near Bimini in the Bahamas, "under the slime of ages of seawater." In 1940 he predicted that "Poseidia will be among the first portions of Atlantis to rise again. Expect it in '68 and '69; not so far away." No remains heaved up from the seabed at the predicted time, but in 1968 stone formations suggesting the outlines of pyramids, roads, walls, and circles were found on the ocean floor near

Bimini. Some people believe they are the ruins of Atlantis.

Cayce was of the opinion that many Atlanteans have been reincarnating recently, in America in particular—a nation that wields great power in the form of the atom bomb and enjoys advanced technology. It is also a society of chaos unbalanced by the effects of greed, materialism, violence, and the desire for instant gratification of the senses at the expense of our neighbors and our home, the earth. We are now facing the same choices between spirit and matter, the good and the profane, that the Atlanteans reportedly did. Atlantean past-life regressions call attention to these choices: to the potential of power used for good, the terrible results of power abused, and the need for spiritual growth.

ATLANTEAN REGRESSIONS

Descriptions of Atlantis from past-life regressions by widely disparate sources bear striking similarities. In general, they support the Cayce readings. At its best, Atlantis emerges as a land of light and crystal, with great, glistening temples and crystalline pathways. The air is moist and silky, the gardens lush, and the environment unpolluted. The people communicate telepathically. At its worst, Atlantis suffers from a population explosion, with overcrowded cities and a polluted environment, and from social and political turmoil.

Some people, when they first see such scenes in their regressions, think they are in a classical setting, in Greece or Rome, perhaps, though they recognize that there is something strange and different about their surroundings. One man said:

There was a predominance of white, especially in clothing, which was soft and flowing. A lot of people wore white headbands. The whole area was extremely clean, and was contemporary but not like we know it.

Another description was given by a woman:

There were pyramids that were centers of great energy, like power plants. Only certain people were allowed inside—engineers and technicians, I suppose, and officials. I also saw temples with huge columns. I thought I was in ancient Greece, but the thought came into my head that, no, this was Atlantis. I didn't want to believe it at first. The air was very moist, a marine climate. There weren't any cars that traveled on land. Instead, people drove around through the sky in little vehicles not much bigger than a motorcycle side-car with no wheels.

Many Atlantean recalls also concern the highly developed technology, for example, airships that traveled on crystal power or magnetic force. One young woman gave this description of her life in Atlantis just before and during its final destruction:

I saw myself in a temple at the age of fourteen, being tutored in spiritual matters. At first I thought I was in ancient Egypt or Greece because of the temples and statues, although they were unlike anything I'd ever seen before. Then it came to me that I was in Atlantis. After my tutoring, I went out with a group of friends. We were picked up by others in a strange vehicle that didn't have wheels but floated along. The funny thing about regressions is you can't change them. Now, I'm a pretty rational person, and in my mind, I kept trying to put wheels on the car, to make the picture something I could cope with. But I couldn't change the picture.

We all got into this car and went to a mountain and sat on top of it. There were six of us and we sat in a circle, practicing mental telepathy. We looked at each other, thinking things and trying to communicate them telepathically. [The regressionist] asked, "What are you thinking about?" and I said, "What's for dinner!" We were typical fourteen-year-olds just being silly.

I progressed a few years into the future and saw that I and my friends were learning how to rule. Then I progressed and saw the destruction of Atlantis. I was about fifty years old when everything fell down and exploded. At the time, I was a member of a governing body with these other people. I knew that somebody was abusing their power and that something awful was about to happen, and it did. Everything blew up and collapsed. I was in an office. Huge stones were falling and I knew I was going to be crushed. I left my body seconds before it was hit by a falling building. I felt I had chosen the time to leave. I saw myself leave my body.

Dick Sutphen, who has done regression seminars all over the country, has found that when he asks others to return to a life in Atlantis if they had one, most people are able to do so. That would support Cayce's belief that reincarnating Atlanteans are gravitating to America. Those persons who have little or no conscious knowledge of Atlantis often see a wealth of detail that corroborates other accounts. Writing in his book *Past Lives, Future Lives*, Sutphen said, "I believe most of us now living in the United States are ex-

Atlantians [*sic*] who have returned at this time because we function well in the accelerated vibrations of an advanced age."

In the same book, Sutphen tells of an Atlantean regression experienced by his former wife, Trenna, in which she observed herself and Sutphen as young graduates of the School of Philosophy, an ancient school well entrenched in society but resented by the ruling elite. Knowledge of past lives was general among the population, and a history of the proper incarnations was required for admission to the college. Trenna and Sutphen trained for spiritual work and married. Trenna described their odd wedding, in which the two met in a chamber where there were large pieces of round silver metal. With their minds, they caused the discs to vibrate, creating a harmony that joined their two spirits together. They thus were empowered to communicate mentally over great distances, creating as well a healing color for use in their spiritual work.

Out in the field, they promoted education among the downtrodden lower classes and were accused of inciting the masses to revolt. They returned to their school, in a temple high on a hill overlooking a city, to discuss their work with their professor. They considered taking their vehicle over the mountains to work with primitive people. The vehicle was disc-shaped and could accommodate two persons. It hovered about four feet off the ground by reversing gravity, but had no great power.

Before they could leave, however, a seer warned of impending disaster to the city. A tidal wave struck and hordes of panic-stricken people tried to flee inland as the city was destroyed. Trenna and Sutphen felt the people's fear as vibrations through the skin. Those in the temple knew the water would rise to destroy it as well. Knowing they were doomed, Trenna and Sutphen left their bodies and went to the spiritual plane.

Another story involving the technology and corruption in the waning days of Atlantis was given to me by a West Coast woman in her late thirties who suffered from a common phobia.

I've always had a horrible fear of flying. My panic attacks were so bad that they affected my life. I never would have *remotely* considered a job that required frequent flying, and the small amount of flying I've had to do for business has been extremely difficult for me to undertake. Days before I was scheduled to fly, I would begin to have anxiety attacks and nightmares of the plane crashing. The day of the flight, I had diarrhea and couldn't eat. I prayed desperately for protection. When I got on board, I was your worst case of white-knuckle flier, clutching the armrests the whole way. I suffered heart palpitations. The slightest change in the engine noise would send my pulse rate soaring. I would flag down the stewardess and ask her if we were "safe." I tried deadening myself with alcohol, but it didn't help. I tried to knock myself out with tranquilizers and sleeping pills, but they didn't work, either. A flight across the country seemed like eternity, and it was agony all the way. More than once, I chickened out and came up with an excuse not to go. Or I would fly out and then be too paralyzed to fly back, and end up taking the bus or train home.

I know a lot of people are afraid of flying, but the extreme nature of my fear seemed irrational. Only once in my life was I ever on a really bumpy flight, and I've never been on a plane that had serious mechanical difficulties. I began to wonder if my fear was connected to a past life. If I had to imagine one, I would have guessed that I'd died in a plane crash in either World War I or World War II—that would have made the most sense to me.

I went to see a regressionist. I found that I had indeed died in a plane crash, though the vehicle I saw wasn't really a plane, or anything that we would call a plane. It was a soft oval shape with no wings, rather like a blimp in shape but with no compartment underneath. It was a light gray in color and had windows, and was smaller than a jetliner. It seemed to move along on some sort of energy patterns.

I was a man in my forties. I was lean and dark-haired and had very intense eyes. I was a politician or government official of some sort. I was very controversial, but had a wide following among the people. It seemed that there was a lot of political upheaval, and I had a lot of enemies in high places. My job required me to spend a lot of time traveling around the land. There were death threats against me. I traveled anyway, because I was very concerned about the evil and corruption I saw around me, and I felt I had to fight against it.

My airship was sabotaged by enemies. There was an explosion and then it went down. At the moment I died, I knew it was sabotage and not an accident, and I was filled with anger and resentment, both at dying while I still had important work to do, and at leaving behind my wife and children.

The regression explained a curious thing to me about my present fear of flying. Part of the fear was that the plane would be sabotaged somehow. This was in the days before terrorist attacks on planes, so there was no reason to think that some-body would blow up an airplane.

Afterward, my fear of flying lessened. It has not gone away completely, but at least I can get on a plane now without great anxiety and without pills. I'm no longer an emotional basket case about it.

We may never know for certain when and how Atlantis perished, or even if it existed. However, Atlantis can still be meaningful in past-life recall. The lost continent most often comes up in regressions in which individuals are searching for information to improve their present lives. In that respect, the question that needs to be asked is, "What does Atlantis represent to me?" In other words, Atlantis should be regarded as an archetype.

Archetypes are primordial images, memories, and mental patterns that lie deep within the human psyche in a reservoir that Carl Jung called the "collective unconscious." The collective unconscious is shared by cultures, races, ethnic groups—all of mankind since its beginning. Archetypes are predispositions toward certain behaviors. According to Jung, there is no limit to the number possible for they are created out of the fabric of human experience and the endless repetition of countless situations. In myths and fairy tales, archetypal traits are represented by such figures as the wise old man, the nurturing mother, the hero, the ruler, the trickster, and others. Archetypes and the collective unconscious exist below the level of the conscious mind, yet permeate and affect it through symbols, dreams, and intuitive and inspired thought. It is possible that they surface in past-life regressions as well.

Perhaps Atlantis exists in the collective unconscious as a group of archetypes. To some individuals, Atlantis represents healing powers and psychic development, while to others it represents the danger of apathy and spiritual death, the abuse of power, or the misuse of technology.

CHAPTER SEVEN

Karmic Ties to Others

As we go around the wheel of rebirth, we make our journeys with souls we have known before. More than likely, we have spent multiple lifetimes (but not necessarily *every* lifetime) with the persons who are closest to us in the present: spouse, lover, family, friends, even close business associates. We may have changed our sexes and changed our roles, and some of our present relationship problems—and our present happiness—are the products of what happened before. We also may meet our enemies and those we do not like over and over again. In all relationships, the ideal is to work out problems and achieve harmony.

We decide our reunions and roles before we come back in the flesh. The choices are said to be dictated by karma: the unfinished business of the past and the lessons we are attempting to master on the physical plane. Perhaps we are part of a soul group that has agreed to return at certain periods in time.

Some of our incarnations bring us together with "soul mates." Definitions of a soul mate vary, though according to one definition, each soul has only one soul mate, a true love and other half, for all of eternity. Such a soul mate exists in a marital or lover relationship. More likely, one may have any number of soul mates to whom one grows especially close, and with whom one can be a spouse, lover, friend, or family member. We may choose to live at a time when we can encounter one or more soul mates in different relationships in the same life.

Too much emphasis has been placed upon finding soul mates as an end unto itself. We should not be making our way through life forever worrying that we are missing out because we have not found our soul mates. Reincarnation is the evolution of Self. In the course of that evolution, we are aided—and hindered—by other souls, some of whom join us in many lifetimes. The ultimate goal is to shed our imperfections and conquer desire and ego to become self-realized, a state in which we are complete unto ourselves and are reunited with God.

By no means should anyone seeking a soul mate be discouraged from doing so. Soul mates, after all, may be an important part of the growth process. If we are lucky enough to have a relationship with a soul mate, and even luckier to recognize it, so much the better. Soul mates, however, must be put in perspective: they are only a part of the picture.

There is some evidence demonstrating how intense desires influence our life choices. Two of Ian Stevenson's cases among the Tlingit of southeastern Alaska involve reincarnation choices made before death, which were announced to others. One case involved William George, a fisherman who wanted to be reborn into his own family. In 1949, he gave his favorite son his gold watch and said he would be reborn with him. They would recognize him by the same birthmarks he had, on the left forearm and shoulder. Shortly thereafter, the sixty-year-old man disappeared with his boat, and his body was not found. Slightly more than nine months later, his daughter-in-law gave birth to a boy, her ninth child. The birth was preceded by a dream in which William George appeared to her and said he was waiting to see his son. The baby was born with birthmarks in the same spots as William George's. Little George Jr., as he was named, bore a striking resemblance to his dead grandfather. As he grew older, he called his aunts and uncles his daughters and sons. At age five, he found the gold watch and declared it was his.

The second case took place in 1946–47. Victor Vincent, a stutterer, told his favorite niece, a Mrs. Chotkin, that he would be reborn as her son, and that he would bear the same scars he had then, one on his nose and one on his backside, which was a surgical scar. Vincent said he hoped he would not stutter so badly. He died in the spring of 1946. About eighteen months later, Mrs. Chotkin had a baby boy, Corliss Jr. The baby bore scars in the same spots as Vincent, and the one on his backside resembled a surgical scar. At thirteen months, he told his mother he was "Kahkody," Vincent's tribal name. By age three, Corliss recognized persons known to Vincent. He stuttered until he was nine years old, and demonstrated the same skill with engines that had been possessed by his uncle.

This chapter and the next look at different ways that karma ties us to others.

She Returned as Her Granddaughter-in-Law

Barbara Hand Clow is well known in Age of New Consciousness and publishing circles. With her husband, Gerry Clow, she runs Bear & Co., a thriving publishing house in Santa Fe, New Mexico, with a wide range of titles in religion, ecology, philosophy, psychology, healing, mysticism, and spiritual development. She also works as an astrological counselor. In 1982, Clow undertook a remarkable journey into her own past. For two years she worked with hypnotherapist Gregory Paxson, exploring numerous past lives in order to discover herself and her true purpose, as well as for research toward her master's thesis. Her odyssey spanned 12,000 years of human history, taking her from the depths of intense pain and anguish to soaring heights of ecstasy and enlightenment. She experienced lives of dullness and misery, and lives of wonder in which she served, in both male and female forms, in the priesthoods of the ancient Egyptians, Druids, and Greeks.

Clow published her account of her journey as *Eye of the Centaur: A Visionary Guide into Past Lives* and *Heart of the Christos: Starseeding from the Pleiades*, the first two books of a trilogy called *The Mind Chronicles*. For this book, she discussed new insights and revelations about her karma with others arising from her past-life experiences.

From childhood, Clow has always had a strong sense of living in other times and places. As a young girl growing up in Saginaw, Michigan, her hometown, and in New York City, her other-life memories interfered with her ability to live in the present.

As far as my parents were concerned, I did a lot of inexplicable things, like being able to read Egyptian hieroglyphics and symbology when I was five years old. What explains a five-year-old who wants to study *The Egyptian Book of the Dead?* I had a very unusual interest in ancient cultures, and I studied them intensely. I didn't feel like I fit in my small Midwestern town. I felt like I'd been dropped out of a plane and just landed someplace. Gradually I oriented myself. I was very close to my grandmother, who acquainted me with the fairies. I was taught very early to see the unseen, and I've retained that ability. I've always had a very strong sense of other worlds, other dimensions being present with me all the time. I've often experienced déjà vu. There were voices within me clamoring to be recognized.

I was raped when I was two years old—I didn't know this until February 1988, when I uncovered it during an all-day "deep talking" therapy session. During World War II, I was sent away to live with friends in a small town in northern Michigan because my mother couldn't take care of me. The woman wanted to make sure that my mother didn't find out about the rape, so she spent the next six months to a year after it happened, while she was caring for me, convincing me that I did not know what had happened. I was subjected to a verbal campaign that what I had experienced was not real. I did "forget," but it left an ugly trauma inside.

I was a very complex, disturbed child. Dealing with reality was overwhelming, and I tried to commit suicide when I was five and again at seventeen.

Clow married at nineteen and had two children. By 1972, at age twenty-nine, she was divorced and supporting her children alone. She married her second husband and had two more children. She worked as a Jungian-oriented astrological counselor. Her life revolved around taking care of others. By age thirty-eight, her internal ferment had reached high pressure and Clow had what she described as "a classic midlife crisis":

I was going crazy. I had never been able to find my purpose and a way to express myself. I felt empty inside. These inner voices, these beings were screaming for identification. I needed to finally do something for myself. I began past-life regression therapy with Gregory Paxson, but discovered that it was not enough. I went to my husband and I said, "We've got two choices here: a mental institution or graduate school. I think graduate school is the better choice." He agreed. I enrolled in Mundelein College in a demanding program then run by Matthew Fox, the controversial Dominican theologian who was silenced by the Vatican in 1988. After I was in school for one month, my husband quit his job and stayed home to take care of everything.

I continued to have two regressions each month while I studied at school. I began to see that the regressions were similar to Jungian analysis in terms of the material I was accessing. As a result, my master's thesis was "A Comparison of Jungian Psychoanalytic Technique and Past-Life Regression Therapy," which provided the genesis for *Eye of the Centaur* and *Heart of the Christos*.

It didn't matter to me whether I was looking at real past lives or expressions of subconscious need. What was important was the transformation that began to take place deep inside me.

The first regression was very traumatic. I was an Assyrian woman, Lydia, who was raped as a teen. A group of men grabbed me behind a building in Lastra, where I lived, and raped me. The pain was unbelievable. My little brother, who was with me, tried to stop them, but they hit him and pulled him away. I dragged myself home, only to face my father's fury. My brother and I had been going somewhere we were not supposed to go. My mother was very sad. It was essentially the end of life for me. I was soiled, unfit for marriage, and in that culture could only become a prostitute, walking the streets with my head shrouded, a fallen woman, dirty and miserable, nothing but a commodity.

I later discovered that my mother, father, and brother in that life are my present mother, father, and brother. There's a strong tendency in regression therapy to first pick up lives that concern the primary figures in your current life, such as your parents, your spouse, whoever. That regression enabled me to let go of my emotions about the sexual abuse I'd suffered. I also think it helped me later to integrate the discovery of early childhood rape in this lifetime. The memory of Lydia came in 1982, and I recovered the memory of the rape in this lifetime in 1988. The psyche carefully accesses what it can integrate at a given time. I don't see any karmic connection between the two rapes, however. I think most women will encounter rapes when they assess past lives.

During the process of regression, I found that after going deep within my emotional body to release trauma, I could then access some lifetime of amazingly high consciousness and development, which has in turn been valuable in this lifetime. This has been a pattern throughout all my regressions: release of pain to achieve higher wisdom. When I am willing to go into the shadow and the deep of myself, then the reward comes. I have re-accessed teaching techniques, healing techniques, and sophisticated techniques of emotional bonding with other people, but only after facing the pain and darkness.

The fifth life Clow experienced was her most recent past incarnation, as a Victorian woman who died of cancer in 1932. She was wealthy and lived in a large corner house in Chicago. In appearance, she was plain: tall and bony in build, with a large nose that had a bump on the ridge, brown hair, and soft, loose skin. Her life was one of great emptiness, for despite her wealth, she felt imprisoned and isolated. The care of her children and all decisions regarding them were controlled by her husband's mother, who thought her daughter-in-law would be a bad influence on them. The Victorian woman felt useless and resented her husband and mother-in-law, but she did not resist them. Instead, her rage turned inward, and her body was consumed by cancer. She died at the age of forty-six, resigned and apathetic, with her eight-year-old daughter looking on.

As Clow experienced this life, she suddenly realized the woman had been *her grandmother-in-law*. Now she understood why she bore a striking physical resemblance to her late grandmother-in-law that astonished others, and why her own relationship with her mother-in-law was so unusual. Clow related:

When I met my second husband, I was a twenty-nine-year-old single woman with two children, and was not the best choice for a well-educated young man from a very well-to-do family. Yet I received complete acceptance from his mother and her brother, both of whom might have been expected to oppose this match. When we became engaged, my future mother-in-law gave me a diamond and onyx pin that had belonged to her mother. When she handed it to me, it was like somebody was handing me a watch that I had worn for fifteen years—it felt like *my* pin.

Other unusual things happened in my relationship with her. I always felt like I was older and wiser than her, but I never could understand it. She had a profound, strong, and loving emotional connection to me.

Before I began regressions, I had a difficult time not being judgmental with some of my astrology clients. It was a serious flaw and hindered my work as a healer and teacher. Now I could see that the judgment was coming from this Victorian woman. She was inside me like an inner being, creating some kind of intercellular resonant field in my physical body.

I was able to work on it and release the negative energy. The judgmental person inside me left. For about three weeks after the regression, I could feel these gray waves going out of me. They were like spiderwebs of stickiness. I could feel them literally leaving my body, particularly from my shoulders. It was like a shadow that had been clutching me all those years was gone. From then on I was able to deal with all my clients with an open heart and compassion.

I couldn't discuss this with my mother-in-law because her religious beliefs do not include reincarnation. But my relationship with her and my compassion for her deepened tremendously. She was the little girl with blue eyes I'd seen at the Victorian woman's deathbed. Still I wake up at night seeing her blue eyes. A part of her died when her mother did. Her mother's soul was imprisoned to hover near earth until she was reincarnated as me, eleven years later in 1943, to find her daughter again.

For Clow, as is often the case, the most recent past life was the most unresolved. While Clow was able to release her negative emotions, she sensed that she was still carrying negative physical karma related to the Victorian woman's cancer.

She died when she was forty-six and left behind four small children and a husband. There I was, thirty-eight and the mother of four children. I wondered what would happen to me when I turned forty-six. I was watchful about that. In November before my forty-third birthday, which is February 14, I was told by my gynecologist that I needed to have a hysterectomy. My grandmother-in-law had died of uterine cancer. I sought a second diagnosis, and the need for a hysterectomy was confirmed. I had no signs of cancer, but I worried that I would die in surgery or that cancer would be discovered. I scheduled the surgery for February 27 because I was too busy to do it before then.

Around January 1, I thought I'd better check into the matter. I was seeing Chris Griscom. I said, "Chris, I think we'd better go into the Higher Self, go deep inside, and see if there's anything going on that we don't know about." Chris agreed.

Chris's healing work focuses on the emotional body, which is the part of us that holds feelings and experiences. Using acupuncture, she put me in a light state of hypnosis. She started working on my head with her fingers. A voice came through, which is very unusual for me—I don't channel. The voice said, "You must have this surgery between your birthday and her birthday of your forty-third year. If you do not have the surgery at that time, you will die of uterine cancer."

I didn't know when my grandmother-in-law's birthday was. I went home and got out her biography and found it was March 19. I had scheduled the surgery exactly between our birthdays.

I elected to have local anesthesia during the surgery so that I could be totally conscious and aware, so that I would not have any astral body invasion. Two days after the surgery, my gynecologist said to me, "We've gotten the results from your lab test, and you have a rare form of endometrial tumors developing. They're not cancerous at this time, but they form first as tumors and then become cancerous. They're a very fast-developing form of cancer, and detectable only by Pap smear. If you had not come in for a hysterectomy now, you would have had cancer by summer and you wouldn't have known it without a Pap smear. You could have died."

I passed the point when she probably first got cancer, when she was forty-three. If I had not had the hysterectomy, I think I would have faced dying from cancer at the same age she did—forty-six. I have now passed her death point at age forty-six, and the imprint of her on my physical body is totally gone. She was with me all the way through my forty-sixth year.

Following her regression sessions, Clow began the task of integrating them all into her consciousness. After completion of her graduate studies, she and her husband went to work at Bear & Co. Clow saw immediate improvements in all facets of her life, in home, work, and self. Her therapist, Gregory Paxson, observed in *Eye of the Centaur* that lifetimes are interactive and, with the collaboration of the Higher Self, contribute to the refinement of energy of the whole being. Clow, he said, "is and is not the woman I first met in 1982, or perhaps I should say she is a very different manifestation of that woman. She has worked through many goals, exploring, releasing, expanding, and moving deeper into the energies and nature of her being.''

Clow remains uncertain that all or even some of the past lives she saw were "real," but feels no doubt that the benefits of those experiences are very real:

> I am happier and feel more balanced. I am content in my own body, my own being. I don't think very many people feel that way. Before, I was "dead" and didn't know it. If you allow yourself to go to the deepest place of pain and the highest place of ecstasy, what you get is your energy back. I am now capable of an unbelievable amount of work. I write a book every eighteen months, I am an editor, I've got four kids, and I have a therapeutic practice. Up until age thirty-seven, I was depressed, with a tremendous amount of nervous energy that was not productive.

CARETAKER OF THE HEART

Sometimes karmic ties appear unexpectedly in regressions. We see the same people from our present playing different roles in our past. Suddenly we see our relationships—and ourselves—from new perspectives.

When a friend convinced Laurel Powers to try past-life regression, Powers agreed only with the greatest skepticism. Powers, who works as a mortgage banker in Houston, was dubious about reincarnation. Even if it were true, she wondered what possible benefit there would be in looking at past lives—they certainly couldn't change the present. She had read a few articles on the subject and knew all about Shirley Mac-

Laine's experiences, but past lives still seemed intangible and very remote from day-to-day living.

In the spring of 1988, Powers's friend took her to one of Houston hypnotherapist Sandee Mac's small group regression sessions. Mac's approach (see Chapter Three) is to devote a session to a theme, such as a life in ancient times or a life of importance. The past-life explorers visualize a tunnel, then step out of it and into a past life. Each person examines his or her appearance and views the life from various perspectives: youth, at moments of significance, old age, and death. Then the present self is introduced to the past self so that useful information may be transmitted to help resolve current problems.

Powers didn't expect to get much out of a regression but thought that at the very least the evening would be entertaining. She was so surprised by her vivid experience that she explored several other past lives in subsequent sessions. She was even more surprised at the beneficial energy released by getting in touch with her past. What she learned allowed her to see her present relationships in a new light, empowered her with great self-confidence, and enabled her to achieve a dramatic loss in weight of more than 120 pounds.

I had never been hypnotized before. The theme was life in an early culture. I stepped out of the tunnel and knew immediately that I was male, which was something of a shock. I just didn't expect that. I had a completely different physical appearance, that is, I wasn't overweight. I *knew* it was me standing there, even though I looked so different. I began to get images that I was outside in a very dry, sandy, almost desertlike environment. There was a village with little huts.

It was surprising how clearly things came to me about myself. It was very vivid, like watching a movie. I was totally *there*. The time period seemed to be the 500s—I'm not sure. I was a shepherd, maybe fifteen or sixteen years old. I could see my sheep. I was average height and had long brown hair and white skin that had turned really tan. I had an ordinary life. My home was a small hut with a shelf or bunklike bed built into the wall and very bare furnishings. The hut appeared to be made out of stucco, sand, or brick—it was built out of materials from the surrounding terrain. I lived alone. There never were other people involved in my life, no spouse or kids. It seemed to be a peaceful, uneventful life. I died of old age in my bed.

When Sandee introduced the me now to the me then, it was a comforting situation. The two images embraced. The message was that everything was going to be okay, that I'll be able to take care of myself and won't be unhappy by doing so. I won't need somebody else to take care of me. It all was really clear to me, undeniable that this really had happened. It was just like my own memories.

After that, I was really hooked on seeing more past lives. You begin to sort of doubt yourself, though, like you've seen too many movies and you're prompting yourself. But because of the integrity of the way the sessions were conducted, and the fact that the experiences of others in the group were so diverse, it gave me a lot of confidence that I wasn't making it up and Sandee wasn't leading us.

I have a really close friend who is English, and he turns up a lot in my past lives. I've only known Simon a little over a year, but when I first met him, we developed a close relationship in a hurry; I really clicked with him. In these past-life experiences, sometimes he's male, sometimes he's female, and he takes on different roles: a central character or a minor part of my life, or maybe a presence in a crowd.

I have another really close friend whom I've known almost all my life, Leslie, and she turns up a lot as well. She's always a child of mine and I'm charged with taking care of her. I find that interesting, because in our relationship in the present I feel very protective and responsible for her well-being.

The topic one night at Sandee's was to experience a life in which someone in our present was involved. My intention was to find out about Simon. I found myself in London at around the turn of the [twentieth] century. I was a fairly young man in an ordinary sort of life. I worked in some kind of trade and made a modest living. The most vivid thing that happened in this life was my marriage. It was a big festivity. I saw myself standing there getting married. A man who is not known to me now was giving away the bride, whom I recognized as Simon. [As a woman] she was small and attractive and had blond hair. I was average-looking, brown hair, nothing especially noticeable.

I was propelled forward beyond the wedding and went into the future a few years. We'd had a child, a girl—it was Leslie. I moved forward in time again and became aware that my wife had died and I still had this child to raise. I went on into the future and observed that the child had died as well; I saw her in her coffin at the funeral. She was maybe eight or nine years old. The feeling I had was a sense of release from the worry and responsibility. I didn't feel a lot of emotion, but I seem to be emotionally detached in all the regressions. I died of old age.

The message I got after meeting myself in this life was one of having a sense of duty and responsibility that I have to take care of things. Again, that's the way I feel now, to some extent.

In another session, we were to pick a time period of interest to us. This was very intriguing to me, because I was a history major in college. I picked the Middle Ages. We were also supposed to view an influential life, one in which we were powerful.

I turned up in England again. In all the regressions I've done so far, I've only been female once, and that was in this medieval English life. I was a sorceress and I seemed to be involved in alchemy. I was a small person with long brown hair. I was wearing a long blue dress. I seemed to be fairly affluent, and lived in what looked like a castle. It had banners flying off the top and flags. It was dark inside. I spent most of my time in a laboratory, working on this alchemy. It wasn't witchcraft, it was more of a scientific nature. For some reason, I had to work in secret and keep it really quiet.

Evidently the secrecy didn't work out. As I moved forward in time, I suddenly got a strong smell that was dank, musty, and kind of nasty. I thought it actually came over the room I was in [for the regression]. I didn't know what it was. Then I realized that it was part of the past life— that I was now in a dungeon, imprisoned for my activities. I was held for many years and died there alone.

Simon was in that life—he was somebody who was working with me. We didn't have a close relationship, and he wasn't in prison.

The message from that life was a sense of power and ability. I had power that other people didn't know about; it was my secret. And even though I was discovered and imprisoned, no one ever found out my secrets—they died with me.

In analyzing several regressions, Powers observed:

I've had plain lives. I'm often solitary and alone, though I'm aware of people in the distance. In the lives I've seen, I've just died of old age—I haven't had any accidents or trauma or sickness. Very often I appear the same in old age from life to life, though I don't appear the same during the earlier parts of those lives. I'm usually a man, and have long gray hair and a long gray beard. I'm dressed in a robelike garment rather than clothes that were appropriate to the time. Some sessions I didn't get much out of, and I think it was because I didn't have a life that was relevant to the topic.

After viewing several lives, Powers attended a session devoted to "most powerful life." The setting that emerged for her was modern, which was confusing. Yet themes from her past and present were crystallized in powerful and moving imagery.

In the other regressions, I was always outdoors when I came out of the tunnel. This time, I saw a lot of light, but it was artificial. I kept trying to say, "No, you're not seeing that correctly." A few seconds went by, and the image came to me— I realized it was the light of a surgical room, those bright lights that shine over the operating table. I was male and a surgeon. I looked down and observed my feet—I had on those little slippers that look like green shower caps. As the image became clearer, I saw I was operating on someone, a woman. I knew it was Leslie.

I was in a surgical amphitheater, and up above were students looking down, watching me. Simon was one of them. I was doing heart surgery. I was actually removing the heart from the patient. I took it out, and as I held her heart, it became a piece of rose quartz. That was the last image I had.

It seemed like the United States and very current. That's what puzzled me—it didn't seem like a past life at all. There was nothing gruesome or violent about it. It wasn't frightening to me, but again, the message was one of my responsibility for protecting Leslie and taking care of her heart.

Asking what she has learned overall from these experiences, Powers summed up:

The recurrent theme is that I can take care of myself—that I have to take care of myself. I may very well be called on to take care of other people, but I'll be okay on my own. There's a sense of being alone—not lonely, but alone. And that things are within my power to control. There's also a recurrent sense that if I take charge and do things, they will turn out well, that I can better my situation and be free of problems.

I feel stronger and have a better sense of overall well-being. I feel more secure with myself now. That's something I was never very good about. I try to take responsibility for things and make sure they go well, but previously I didn't necessarily think that I could do it on my own. I used to feel pretty dependent on other people, and now I don't feel that way as much.

[The regressions] definitely enhanced my relationships with others. I see and understand things more clearly. I have better intuition. I don't have to spend a lot of time on the getting-to-know-you part. Things that are more important come out more quickly. I don't waste time with situations or people that aren't going to mean a lot to me.

My weight loss was in a way a result of this. I have always been overweight and I thought I would always be that way, that I didn't have the willpower or whatever it took to do anything about it. But realizing that I can take control of things in my life made me think I could lose weight, too. I knew if I could do that, I could do anything. I came to past-life regression with a lot of skepticism, but now I believe reincarnation is undeniable.

CHAPTER EIGHT

Keeper of the Jim Morrison Flame

At the age of twelve, Danny Sugerman was a restless Los Angeles youth sitting on a powder keg of pent-up energy, looking for direction and a hero. He found both in Jim Morrison, the brilliant but tormented leader of the Doors, whose mystical union of poetry and music pushed out the frontiers of rock. The year was 1967, and the Doors had just burst into international fame with their first hit, "Light My Fire." Sugerman was quickly drawn into the Doors' inner circle as employee, friend, and confidante. It seemed like a lucky break then, but Sugerman would find out years later that meeting up with Morrison and the Doors was no accident, but the continuation of a karmic dance that had begun centuries earlier.

By 1967, Morrison was plunging headlong into a psychedelic quest for higher consciousness and the Universal Mind. An intellectual man, he introduced others around him, including Sugerman, to philosophy and poetry, drugs, and the pursuit of enlightenment and, as he quoted from Norman O. Brown, "unendurable pleasure infinitely prolonged." The Quest for Consciousness became not only the driving creative force of the Doors' music but a way of life. By July 1971, Morrison was dead in Paris, burned out at the age of twenty-seven. Officially, his death was attributed to natural causes, but his legendary drinking and drug use were whispered to have been contributing factors.

Sugerman subsequently played a key role in keeping the spirit of Morrison and the Doors alive, assuming management of their catalogue of LP's and the career of keyboard player Ray Manzarek, his close friend. With rock writer Jerry Hopkins, he co-wrote a best-selling biography of Morrison, *No One Here Gets Out Alive*.

Sugerman's own quest for higher consciousness led him into drug addiction, however, and he struggled against the problem for years. In his effort to find answers and solutions, he undertook a journey into past lives, in which he discovered karmic connections with both Morrison and Manzarek. In an interview, Sugerman said of his experience:

Back in the good old days before bad habits became addictions, I was taking drugs on a fairly regular basis from the time I met Jim Morrison in 1967. I met him through a Little League baseball game. This guy was umping for a little extra money, but what he really did was road-manage his neighbor's rock band, the Doors. I'd seen the equipment that he carried around in the back of his VW microbus. I had been nagging him to take me to see the band. Then one day he said, "If you hit a home run, I'll take you to see the Doors." So I did.

The concert changed my life. It was a religious experience for me. Jim believed in the spiritual power of music, the shaman's dance, the power of theater and electricity, the drums-and-rhythm healing ceremony. Or, to use another apt description, he was Dionysus personified. Jim identified with these forces and knew how to use them. It was a really liberating experience for me, and I'm pretty sure it was for others there that night.

Through the roadie, Sugerman got closer to the Doors, particularly Morrison and Manzarek. It wasn't long before he went to work for them.

I knew Jim would not reject me. I was twelve to his twenty-two; he already famous and me still a nobody, but none of that mattered. I started out answering fan letters, doing some press for them—I was an office assistant. He was my hero, like a big brother. I never did get to college. Jim was a college graduate. He once said, "Just because teachers can't teach and school's a drag doesn't mean you shouldn't read books." He was an avid reader. He gave me Aldous Huxley's *The Doors of Perception*, after which the Doors were named, and *Beyond Good and Evil*. I didn't understand all of it, but I understood enough. He gave me [poet Arthur] Rimbaud's life story to read. I identified with Rimbaud because he was nineteen by the time all of his poetry was written and he ran off to Africa. But Jim's knowledge went beyond books. He just had that look. You *knew* he knew. If I saw that look in your eyes— I'd follow you.

I was an obsessive-compulsive hyperactive personality, and when I found something that interested me, I went after it with a single-mindedness that overwhelmed the people around me. Morrison intuitively knew how to direct that energy onto the path of excess, which has no limits. "The road of excess leads to the palace of wisdom," Blake wrote, and Jim truly believed that. By way of Jim's example, my energy became focused, channeled. Everybody up till then had always told me, "Sit down!" and "Shut up!" Not Morrison. He said, "Go! Go! Go for it! Get it while you can!"

During my experimentation with drugs, I discovered opium. I began smoking it and developed a tolerance for it. Then I became addicted and started snorting heroin. Before I knew it, I was shooting heroin and it was a year since I had taken any psychedelics.

Jim started off on acid and ended up on alcohol, which is a painkiller. I think a lot of people with addictive personalities who began with psychedelics and went on to other drugs found that their drugs of choice were alcohol, cocaine, and heroin, which constrict the consciousness. Huxley talks about the "reducing valve" that psychedelics enlarge to give us entrance into the Universal Mind. At first I thought I wanted that reducing valve enlarged, with grass and psychedelics. But that wasn't what I really wanted at all. I wanted the reducing valve constricted—I wanted to think less. I wanted that "falseness of well-being" I'd heard so much about. True or false, who cared? I'd take it. Life was pain and suffering. I wanted to feel good.

Ultimately, I think Jim got to that place, too, where he depended more on alcohol and less on the hallucinogens he had been taking. At first, alcohol stimulates thought and conversation, but ultimately it creates the same thing heroin does:

oblivion. There's a saying that ignorance is bliss. The opium flower provides that blissful ignorance, but it's not really bliss at all. It's really indifference.

But anyway, I was strung out by the time I was twenty. Jim had been dead for four or five years then, and I was managing the Doors' catalogue, which continued to be successful. And I also was taking care of two of my heroes, Ray Manzarek and Iggy Pop. I had a house in the hills and a sports car and a beautiful girlfriend, and I was going to all the parties that I wanted and had free drugs all the time. At first I thought, "This is the life, this is great!" But the truth was, I was scared and very overwhelmed. I didn't know what I was doing. I expected somebody to rap me on the shoulder at any moment and say, "Excuse me, son, we thought you knew what you were doing, you can't have all this."

I got higher and higher and went out less and less until finally I was locked in the house and the only people who were allowed over were drug dealers, and even them I didn't want around because I didn't want to share any of my drugs, and I didn't want any of them to learn what was in my house. I hated and resented them, and they knew it. They also knew I needed them. It was not a fun period, but I couldn't stop.

I tried to kick it a couple of times, but I couldn't. I thought I could control it. I thought, "I can kick it whenever I want, but I just don't want to yet." I'd try to quit again, but then the craving would get unbearable and I'd be back at it within a couple of days. The hell of being clean would become worse than the hell of being strung out, and off I'd go. Eventually I ended up on methadone maintenance.

But one of the things that really did help me for a while was acupuncture. Jerry Hopkins was in my house when I'd stopped [heroin] once, and it was obvious to him something was up. He demanded that I level with him. I did. I told him, "I'm going through drug withdrawal and I'm sick." He asked me if I wanted help, and of course I did. He called a friend of his who's an acupuncturist. The guy turned out to be the Doors' first photographer, and he had been in jail. While in jail, he'd meditated—that was all there was to do, apparently, lots of dead time. He came out remembering a past life as a Chinese acupuncturist. All of his brown hair and his beard had turned white overnight. He took the exam to qualify for an acupuncture license and passed it without studying. Weird story, huh? The thing was, I'd known him before he went in—we'd met once or twice—and he was totally changed. He resonated serenity. I don't know what happened, except that something powerful went down.

So Jerry called him over. He gave me a treatment, and I immediately got better. The withdrawal withdrew! Acupuncture takes care of the craving and sickness by activating the endorphins produced by the pituitary gland. The same ingredient that kills pain cures withdrawal. More of it creates pleasure—the body's own morphine, but a thousand times stronger.

But the next morning I woke up sick again and was about to call my dealer when he [the acupuncturist] showed up at the door. I said, "How did you know I'd need you?" He said, "I figured you'd be ready for either a fix or another treatment." He gave me another treatment, and it worked fine.

I had to go on tour, and as soon as it [heroin]

was around, I got strung out again. About six months later, I contacted the acupuncturist again and asked him for help. He came to see me and said, "Listen, you have some really dark energy with you. It feels like Morrison. I knew Morrison, and I'm telling you, Danny, before I treat you again, for your own good, you'd better go see a psychic and find out what sort of karma of Morrison's you're carrying around with you and why you can't break this chain." I said, "That's a real interesting question." Mainly, I was just interested in getting some more treatment from this guy. There weren't a lot of acupuncturists at that time [1974–75], and I didn't want to go to another one and say, "I'm coming off heroin, treat me."

He took care of me just that once to get me well enough to go see this psychic that he referred me to. She didn't interpret any past lives for me, but told me to go see a regression hypnotist. She told me she couldn't help me, that there was stuff I had to see for myself. So I said, "All right, fine, I'll try it." So she sent me to see this guy up in Topanga Canyon.

I've always been a good hypnotic patient because I'm susceptible to altered states of consciousness. I'm willing to let go, so I can go right into a trance state. That first Doors concert was an example. I was entranced by that hypnotic music and the spell Morrison cast.

The theme of the session was my relationship with Jim Morrison. In one life he was an older brother, in Amsterdam. Our family owned a general store and I worked in it, but he refused to. In another life, we were pirates. There was a lot of looting, pillaging, and raping going on; I had very intense feelings of shame and remorse. I didn't dig it at all. I mean, at that time—I had too much of a conscience to get into it. I tried to stop them and they tortured me. They put some sort of wood down my throat that expanded as they poured water on it, so eventually I choked to death. Jim was really into the pirate's life, and if I remember right, he was my protector, ya know, "The kid doesn't have to do what he doesn't want to do." But Jim got stabbed and died, and then I was fair game. I don't know what the time period was, because I don't have anything to compare it to. I'm not really versed in history.

Then the regressionist told me to go back, back, further back in time. Eventually I saw this floor take shape, a path of stones and pebbles and earth that I couldn't have imagined. The details, the carved craftsmanship, were amazing, beautiful. I saw plumbing and water and an irrigation system, very intricate yet different as well as beautiful. I know nothing about irrigation. I saw meditation gardens with waterfalls. All the water was used very constructively: this going to the washing, this going to the well, that going to the waterfall, that to the garden, and so on. I could hear the water. I could hear the sound of sandals on these rocks that made up the path, the echoing into the hallway. Something inside me said, "This is real, this is not a dream, this isn't your imagination, *this is real.*"

It was somewhere in China on the border near India, up in the hills, totally isolated, way before the Communist invasion, before Christ. I was a young monk, if monk is what you call it. My head wasn't shaved but my hair was very short. We had on these *dhotis* covered by robes, and sandals. The robes seemed light in color, a beige or a grayish beige. I didn't get the sense I was on any religious quest. I had more of a sense that I had been put there by my family. It was something that was expected of me.

Ray was there—he was an elder. Jim was like the abbot, and his body was dying. Several of us were called in. I was Ray's charge now that Jim was dying. Jim said to me, "I want you to take these notebooks, and I want you to make sure that people know what I'm saying. Don't let people interpret me. If you wait and it is passed down by word of mouth, it's going to be misinterpreted. I spent my life writing this, and it's important. If you care about me, which I know you do, you'll pass this on. You'll continue the work and make it yours, and Behari"—that was Ray's name—"will be with you."

I said, "No, I can't do this, I don't want to deal with it." I was a novice and I was too upset by Jim's body dying. "How can you talk about lessons when you're leaving me?" I said. I didn't take the books. I didn't stay. The books said one thing, I don't know what, and the ashram believed another. I split. It was too much for me. I went back to my family.

Afterward, the regressionist wanted me to come back for another session, but I didn't go back. I wasn't ready to own what I knew, what I'd learned. I wasn't done with using drugs, and using wasn't done with me. Ultimately, I just burned out on it. It's not the sort of lesson that you can learn. You either live to get sick of it or you don't. I was lucky I got sick and tired of being sick and tired.

The regression did explain a lot to me about a lot of things, including this recurring dream I'd been having. I could never remember what it was about, except the sensation that I was filled over brimming, beyond pleasure and pain. It was very disturbing and powerful. I'd wake up and feel my jaw shoved open and my head back, like I was drinking something that was incredibly powerful, with some incredible force behind it, that something solid was just pouring down my throat at an incredible rate, overflowing, filling me up. But it was hard [not liquid]. My lower jaw was snapped open and I couldn't use my mouth. When I came to [from the hypnosis], I knew the dream was related to the pirate life: at the moment of release from the body, there was a sense of relief and gratification and pleasure, but at the same time there was this physical pain.

There was another life in which I worked on the Mississippi and was your standard drunk. So what I had to deal with were the residual effects of the life of drinking and the need to satisfy this oral compulsion—I think those two lives concerned basically the same theme—and the fact that I had not taken responsibility. I didn't take responsibility in the monk life with Jim, and I didn't take responsibility in the Amsterdam life. In this life, I *have* to take responsibility, and I'm doing my job. It's nice to know. If I don't [take responsibility], I'm bothered by the possibility, however remote, that I'll have to go through all this again.

I don't disbelieve in reincarnation, but I also think the mind can't help but filter and color these images so that it can relate to them. I don't think all the experiences I had were true reincarnational experiences. I think the gists of them were true, but the mind interprets in a way that it needs to color. It might make one person a boy instead of a girl because it can't relate to a spirit being feminine, for example. However, the feeling I'm left with to this day is that something is there that is very real, very mysterious, and very powerful.

All I'm saying is, this was my experience. I don't find reassurance in the plausibility of reincarnation, I don't derive comfort from the concept of returning again and again to grow and learn, because I'm a slow learner and growing hurts. At the same time, this same knowledge caused me to get on with the work and to stop procrastinating. On the other hand, you can't consciously remember, anyway, so what difference does it make?

Some years after his hypnotic regression, Sugerman met Michael Talbot, the Manhattan author, and the two collaborated on a project. Talbot had powerful memories of having lived long ago as a Tibetan monk. When Sugerman related his own past-life regression and the images of the remote mountain monastery, Talbot felt certain he had been there at the same time as a fellow monk. With the help of Jim Gordon, a past-life psychic, Talbot pieced together details, described below:

Without explaining anything that Danny had told me, I asked Gordon one simple question: Have I had any past-life experiences with a friend of mine named Danny Sugerman? To my surprise, Gordon immediately started telling me more about the past life Danny had described. He didn't mention Morrison by name and only referred to him as the abbot of the monastery. He said the abbot was very old and was dying, and wanted Danny to take charge of a set of sacred books. Gordon then added some information that had not surfaced in Danny's regression. As Gordon explained, there was a controversy over the books because the monks had discovered plants and roots with hallucinogenic properties. One school of thought in the monastery held that drugs should be used for spiritual advancement, and another school held that that was not the proper path. The abbot wanted Danny to take over the books, but Danny was reluctant because he didn't know how he felt about the issue of whether to use drugs to open spiritual doorways. He didn't take the books, and that is why the drug issue bubbled up with him again in this life, because he was still wrestling with the question.

I asked if there was anything I could do for Danny. Gordon alleges that he communicates with the constellation of souls that have contracted to be guides. It's like having a three-party call. Most often they communicate with him via images; occasionally they give him sentences. He said, "They're telling me that no one can do anything for Danny, he has to do it for himself. You made the right choice in that life by not using drugs. You came together in this life so that he could continue to see you making a lot of right choices, and that might possibly help him."

Sugerman did at last "do it" for himself; he kicked his drug habit in 1984, and wrote about his battle with drugs in his second book, *Wonderland Avenue*. He feels he chose to be with Morrison in this life, and has balanced the karma over those ancient notebooks by carrying on the Morrison flame.

I feel I'm about done with it, finally. I've done just about everything I can for Jim. The book I wrote on him introduced him to millions of souls. That feels good to me. I've been involved with bringing out a new poetry album of his—he always wanted to be taken seriously as a poet. He kept a lot of notebooks and journals. In 1986, some previously unknown notebooks of his were discovered. I thought that was interesting, in light of the regression.

The things that Jim knew and what he was able to write about, and the beliefs he had, are not those of a twenty-seven-year-old man. This guy had wisdom at twenty-seven that only a few of us will have, if we're lucky, at eighty-seven. He was a really old soul. And he was not only a good man but a very brave man. He went out on a very precarious limb—he was out there all alone, with no religion to comfort him, no God to have faith in. He tested the bounds of reality in every way. We have the findings. We got Jim's life even as he lost it. The conclusions are all ours to wrestle with. Jim is free. I hope.

CHAPTER NINE

The Karma and Grace of Love and Hate

Edgar Cayce once observed that the scars of wounds created in one lifetime stretch on down the centuries. So, too, do decisions made by the soul—to love another, hate another, or seek revenge against another. Love has its own sweet rewards, as we have seen in Chapter Seven. Love redeems and furthers spiritual growth. The repercussions of hate, guilt, and revenge reverberate in chain reactions through lifetime after lifetime, too, creating more tragedies and disasters, until a lesson is learned and the karma is discharged by love and forgiveness.

THE FIDELITY DILEMMA OF MRS. X

On the surface, Mrs. X appeared to live an enviable life. She possessed the kind of beauty that made others look twice, had been married for eighteen years to a successful businessman, and led a life of material comfort among wealthy friends.

For years, she hid the dark stain that blotted her life, until at age forty-one she consulted Cayce and confessed her troubles.

Her husband was impotent, totally incapable of providing the kind of physical pleasure she desired from him. She loved him deeply, however, and did not want to hurt him by annulling the marriage or divorcing him. At first, she had found outlets for her needs in relationships with other men, before learning how to sublimate her desire through meditation and spiritual study.

The crisis that motivated her to seek out Cayce was the reappearance in her life of an old flame, a man who had loved her from childhood but had lost her to her husband. They were still deeply attracted to one another, and Mrs. X was tempted to have an affair with him. She resisted because her old love was married, too. She knew his wife and did not want to hurt her, either.

Cayce gave Mrs. X a reading. The cause of her husband's sexual impotence went back 600 years and two lifetimes earlier, to the days of the Crusades, Cayce said. Mrs. X had been a woman named Suzanne Mercelieu, married to her present husband. Monsieur Mercelieu was a religious zealot who joined the Crusades. He mistrusted his wife and forced her to wear a chastity belt during his absence to guarantee her fidelity. Suzanne was so resentful of this cruel and uncomfortable prison that she vowed she would someday get even with her husband. She took that resentment and vow to her grave. Two lifetimes later, they had come back like an ugly boomerang. She was, said Cayce, coming face to face with herself.

Essentially, Mrs. X had already overcome much of her negative karma from the past life. She could have indulged in her revenge in the current life by leaving her husband or ridiculing his impotence. Instead, she had stayed married to him out of deep love and had overcome her urges to have relationships with other men. She had resisted entering a potentially destructive affair with her old flame. It was not her place to punish through revenge, for the law of karma had punished her husband with impotence. By forgiving him through unselfish love, Mrs. X was presented an opportunity to allow both of them to grow spiritually.

ANTHONY H. LEARNS THE LAW OF GRACE

The law of karma operates hand in hand with the law of grace, an inner guiding force that prompts a soul to keep improving itself to reach perfection. To right one's wrongs, one must first forgive oneself. At that point, said Cayce, one begins to move under the law of grace.

Anthony H. was a college student in Connecticut before World War II when he fell in love with a young woman, who subsequently dropped him for his best friend. He discovered through readings with Cayce that he had been married twice to this woman in past lives. One of those lives was in ancient Egypt, where she had jilted him for the same man. Their relationship, it seemed, had always been troubled.

Anthony got over his lost love and got on with his life. He married, and in 1944 was drafted to fight in World War II. One of his chief faults was a short temper, which he strove mightily to control. During his military service, he began to suffer a bizarre problem: he would choke on small objects that lodged in his throat—a plum pit, gristle, or a bit of bone. Each time, he was rushed to the hospital.

After the war, while dining with a friend one evening in Manhattan, a chicken bone stuck in his throat and sent him once again to the hospital. He hovered on the edge of consciousness as he was rushed into the operating room and given an anesthetic. As he went under, an angry face framed by dirty, unkempt yellow hair hovered in front of him. Anthony realized, to his astonishment, that it was himself! Suddenly, he was no longer in the hospital, but in surroundings that appeared medieval and Nordic. What was more, he was in the grip of a homicidal rage against a young woman—his wife. He had just discovered her infidelity and was so consumed with hatred that he was on the verge of killing her with his bare hands. The vision ended abruptly.

A few nights later, Anthony dreamed of the medieval woman, who took on the features of the woman who'd jilted him in college. In the dream, he strangled her to death. He woke up in a cold sweat. He knew enough about reincarnation and the laws of karma and grace to realize the implications of the vision and the dream. Mortified, he began praying fervently for forgiveness for himself and the Nordic woman. The prayer seemed to work, for after a while he felt an enormous burden lifted from him.

Several days later, Anthony was surprised to get a telephone call from the long-lost college girlfriend. She was in Manhattan and had thought wistfully of him, and how shabbily she had treated him in college. She hoped he could forgive her. Of course, he told her, with great relief.

The choking emergencies were retribution for Anthony's strangling of his wife in the past life; perhaps one might have eventually claimed his life. His victim had exacted revenge by loving and leaving him, adding the insult of marrying his best friend. For her, it was a hollow victory, for the marriage had ended in divorce. So had her second marriage, and she was lonely and unhappy. Now, having forgiven themselves and each other, they were free of the need to hurt each other again.

The Lives and Murders of Gail Bartley

Gail Bartley's life took a strange downward turn following her divorce in 1981. Despite the trauma of ending a six-year marriage, the signs were positive for new beginnings. Bartley was still young, only 28, and quite attractive. She had long, curly, dark brown hair, expressive brown eyes, and a slender five-foot-five build. She had a stimulating and challenging job as an art director at a Los Angeles advertising agency, which brought her into professional and social contact with scores of interesting people and potential dates. She was her own woman.

So why did she fling herself headlong into an abusive and destructive relationship with a man named Roger (a pseudonym)? For years, Bartley was unable to answer the question and also unable to end the relationship. Finally, after exhausting conventional forms of therapy, Bartley got her answers through past-life regression. She discovered that the seeds had been planted centuries earlier in ancient Rome, and had grown, misshapen, through a series of unhappy lives.

For Bartley, meeting Roger was the beginning of a compulsion. She didn't feel she had known him before, but she felt compelled to become involved with him—against her better judgment. Her mother took an icy dislike to him after one brief meeting, which Bartley found odd. Her mother was not one to make snap judgments about others. And a voice inside Bartley's head kept screaming, "Get away, get away. He hates you. He's trying to destroy you!"

The relationship that developed between Bartley and Roger was one of intense love and hate, and Bartley found herself swinging from one emotional extreme to the other. She suffered from his emotional and verbal abuse and, occasionally, from his physical abuse as well. Once, during a raging argument, Roger wrestled her to the floor and started choking her.

Bartley wondered what was wrong with her. She had lost her self-esteem. Why was she putting up with this? Who needed this pain? She never let anyone treat her so badly before! Where was her pride?

In 1984, Bartley moved to Manhattan to take a job as the art director of a New York ad agency. Roger followed her and wouldn't let go. At last she ended the relationship, but the scars wouldn't heal. She tried counseling and psychotherapy, but nothing worked. She felt low and depressed.

In 1985, the solutions to her dilemma began to materialize. At the time, they seemed to be mysterious coincidences, though Bartley now believes that there are no "coincidences" in life, but synchronistic events that occur at the right time and place.

Her search for meaning led her to several volumes on reincarnation and past-life therapy, which intrigued her. As a child, she had believed in reincarnation, then abandoned the belief when taunted by teenage friends. That had left her without a spiritual rudder, for organized religion had never appealed to her. Now, Bartley felt ready for spiritual growth.

Bartley decided to try past-life regression. But where to find a regressionist? The answer that popped into her head seemed incongruous: *Go to the Pineapple Dance Center.*

The Pineapple Dance Center in Manhattan offered ballet classes, and Bartley had long been interested in taking one. During her lunch hour, she followed her hunch and went to the center. There, on the reception desk, she found a brochure about a Manhattan regressionist, Alice T. (see Chapter Three). Thrilled, Bartley called her and scheduled an appointment.

Upon arriving for her regression, Bartley felt nervous, despite the comfortable surroundings. Nervous anticipation is common, but Alice soon put Bartley at ease by explaining the procedure. First, she would help Bartley relax in a comfortable reclining chair using guided meditation and background music especially designed to synchronize the right and left hemispheres of the brain. The music, Alice explained, would enhance the vividness of the regression. Then Alice would guide Bartley through an imaginary tunnel toward a light at the other end. Upon emerging into the light, Bartley would find herself in a past life. Before Bartley's arrival, Alice had meditated for spiritual guidance, and to surround their working area with a protective white light. Of the many lives that Bartley undoubtedly had experienced, Alice would ask to be guided to the one (or several) that would shed light on Bartley's present situation with Roger. She would see scenes, and move backward and forward in time to significant moments.

Bartley followed Alice's instructions. She closed her eyes, settled back in the easy chair, and let Alice's soothing voice take her through a progressive relaxation. She had no trouble visualizing the tunnel and the bright, white light at the end. But as she moved through the tunnel toward the light, a cold anxiety began to creep into her bones. The hairs on the back of her neck prickled. She felt a profound dread of something unknown. At the end of the tunnel, the light gave way to darkness, and Bartley did not want to step out into it. Alice relaxed her again, and Bartley felt secure enough to move forward.

The scene was eerie. She found herself standing in a bedroom with high ceilings. Her name was Joyce, and she was twenty-three years old. The time seemed to be the 1920s. Her long, straight brown hair fell down her white nightgown. She was barefoot. Part of

Bartley felt as if she were watching a movie, and part of her seemed to be *in* the movie. As she stood in this darkened bedroom, she was filled with apprehension and fear. Its source was the man lying in the bed near her: her husband—the man she now knew as Roger. She watched him get out of bed and approach until he was standing in front of her. Bartley's fear escalated, and she began to hyperventilate. The drama of past love and hate unfolded:

Alice: What do you feel?
Bartley: Really scared. My heart's beating. (She begins to gasp and moan.) I don't believe it!
A: What's happening?
B: He's putting his hands on my throat. (She continues to gasp and hyperventilate.) He's strangling me. I'm dropping to my knees, I can't breathe!
(Alice instructs and calms her so that she can look at the scene and breathe very easily. Bartley gasps for a few more moments, then begins to calm down.)
A: Breathe very easily, very effortlessly. Tell me what's going on now.
B: He's still holding on to my throat, and I'm lying on the floor. He lets go and stands up.
A: Are you in the body or out of the body?
B: I'm in the body. He walks away. (She indicates to Alice that she can breathe again. She watches Joyce sit up, dazed.) I think I'm okay. He goes to the door and walks out and he shuts it. I'm kneeling now and touching my throat. Now I hang my head, and I get up. I'm just standing there. I don't know what to do. (Alice moves Bartley forward a little in time. Bartley sighs.) I'm walking around the room, and I don't know what to do. I'm thinking I want to leave, but I don't know where to go.
A: Stay in this scene until the next time you see your husband.

B: I see him coming up the stairs, it's the same night. I go out in the hall. He has a cold look on his face. I feel hate. I don't know if I say, "I hate you," or if he says, "I hate you." I just feel it. I don't feel as frightened as I did before. He walks by me, back into the room, and shuts the door.

(Alice asks Bartley to move back in time to a scene that will explain why this hate and confrontation developed. Bartley immediately finds herself at a wedding party—her own. She is wearing a beautiful white gown covered with lace. The reception, attended by a large crowd of people, is taking place in the garden of her family's elegant home. Her husband approaches her.)

B: He's pulling me by the hand, and he grabs me around the waist to kiss me. He kisses me. I don't think I like that—he's rough.

A: How long have you know him?

B: Ten years? A long time.

A: Are you in love with him, is he in love with you?

B: No.

A: Why do you marry? Is it an arranged marriage?

B: I don't know. I'm afraid of him.

A: Are you in front of a lot of people when he's kissing you?

B: We're in the garden still, but he has pulled me away from the crowd. I'm pushing him away. I'm saying I want to get back.

A: What does he say?

B: "Bitch."

(Alice asks Bartley to go to the moment at which she agreed to get married. Bartley sees herself in the study of her parents' house, with Joyce's father and her fiancé. Her father is a banker and well-to-do. Her fiancé also comes from a wealthy family.)

B: We're all talking. We're telling him [her father] we're getting married. He doesn't seem very happy, I

133

don't know [why]. He's listening. We're smiling. [My father] says, "He's not right for you, he's not good enough for you."

A: Why doesn't your father think he's the right man for you?

B: He doesn't like him [because] he's irresponsible and he's violent.

A: How do you feel about your fiancé right now?

B: He's exciting, he's passionate, he scares me.

A: Have you made love with him before?

B: No.

A: How does he feel about you?

B: He tells me that he loves me.

A: How much time is it before you get married?

B: A couple of years.

(Alice asks Bartley to move to another scene that will shed light on the relationship. Bartley sees the two of them in a shiny, new yellow convertible, driving along some cliffs near the ocean. It is before they become engaged.)

B: We're driving fast. We're laughing. I kiss him. Our hair is blowing. He puts his arm around me. I love him. We're still driving, he's driving too fast. I ask him to stop, to slow down. He's angry at me for asking him to slow down, and he stops and he gets out of the car and he just stands there and he won't talk to me. I say, "Don't be upset, I only asked you to slow down." He says, "You're trying to dominate me."

(Alice asks Bartley to go to the next significant scene.)

B: We're kissing.

A: How did you make up?

B: He just stopped being angry.

(Bartley moves to another scene. She sees Joyce and her fiancé back in her parents' home, alone having tea. Bartley begins to tense visibly, and Alice relaxes her. Bartley continues with the regression.)

B: I'm telling him I don't think we should get married. He says, "Don't be silly."

A: Why don't you think you should get married?

B: Because I don't like him. He says I'm crazy.

A: Let go of this scene and move forward without pain to the very last day of your life in this incarnation. How old are you?

B: I can't see anything.

A: Is it dark?

B: Yes, I'm young.

A: I'd like you to move backward in time a few moments until it's light enough for you to see.

B: I'm back in the bedroom.

A: How old are you?

B: Twenty-three! (Bartley is surprised—this is where the regression started.)

A: What's happening? Are you alone?

B: (She begins to gasp for breath and cannot answer immediately. Her breath is heavy and labored.) I'm getting scared again.

(Alice instructs her to stay calm and relaxed.)

A: Is he with you?

B: No, I think I hear him downstairs. [Now] he's at the door.

A: Does he say anything?

B: No, he's holding something behind his back.

A: What is it?

B: I don't know. (She begins to gasp again.) He's walking toward me. I think he has a knife, but I don't believe it! (Bartley pauses while she struggles to get control of her anxiety.) He has a knife. He rips my nightgown with it, in the front. I push him away. He just looks at me and he gets real close. (Again Bartley cannot continue. Her heart is pounding. She breathes heavily for a few moments, and Alice helps her to relax.) I'm not sure [what's happening]. I'm not sure . . . he stabs me. I'm standing by the window. I'm holding myself. He's just standing there in shock. I can't talk, I sink to the ground. (Bartley realizes these are her last moments in this life as Joyce. She has been murdered by her husband, the man she now knows as Roger. As she watches herself die, she feels no pain. She feels herself float out of Joyce's dying body, and hover in a corner of the room, looking down on the scene.)

A: Can you see him?

B: He's standing there with the knife looking down at me and then he looks at the knife.

A: What is he feeling?

B: Shock. He throws the knife. He starts to cry. He runs to me and holds me. He's just holding me. (Bartley feels her soul floating away.)

A: Let go of this now and move backward in time. I want to go back to the scene prior to where he murders you, the scene that precipitated this. I want to know specifically what the argument was—the straw that broke the camel's back.

(Bartley sees the two of them at the dinner table.)

B: I'm laughing at him. He's upset about something. I'm being mean. He's saying he doesn't love me, that he has never loved me. He says that I've never loved him.

A: That's when you laugh?

B: Yes.

A: Let go of this scene and let go of this life. I want to go back to the life where we will find the cause of why he murdered you in this life where you were Joyce.

(Bartley releases the memories of Joyce and, guided by Alice, moves through time. She arrives in the life of a seventeen-year-old boy named George, who lives with his mother and ill-tempered, domineering father in a cabin somewhere in the Old West of America, in the late nineteenth century. George is tall and lean, with sandy-colored hair. When Bartley first sees him, he is standing outside the cabin, wearing a long-sleeved red shirt, blue pants, and scuffed boots. It is night, and the crickets are singing. George's mother comes out of the cabin. She is a small woman with gray hair, wearing a light-colored dress.)

B: She puts her arm around me. She asks me why I'm out here alone. I say that it's just a nice night and I wanted to listen to the crickets. My dad appears in the doorway. He says, "Get in!" (George enters the cabin. The interior is bright and cozy, with a fire.) I don't like my father. I don't know [why]. I like my mother. She's afraid of him.

(Alice asks Bartley to move forward or backward in time to a significant scene. She finds George and his father [Roger in this life] camping in the wilderness. A fire blazes at the campsite.)

B: We're drinking coffee. My father is talking. He's angry at me for doing something wrong, something with the horses—I didn't tie them up right. Then I'm in my sleeping bag. I think I hear noises. It's really quiet, but every so often I hear a noise that's not an animal. I think he's digging.

A: What is he digging?

B: (incredulously) A grave, a hole! I think it's for me! (Bartley becomes agitated. Alice pauses to relax her, and asks her to go on.) He hits me in the head with a shovel! I'm already down, I'm in my sleeping bag. It's funny, I'm observing it like I'm out of the body, I'm leaving the body. He throws down the shovel and he drags me to the grave and he puts me in and he covers me up! He's thinking, making up a story about how I died.

A: Does he feel any remorse?

B: No!

(Alice asks Bartley to move to a scene that will shed light on the hatred between George and his father.

Bartley observes George, still seventeen, at a local dance, dancing with a beautiful girl named Sally. He is in love with her and hopes to marry her someday. The music is lively and the crowd is having a good time. George's happiness radiates from Bartley's face.)

A: You look like you're very happy. I'd like you to enjoy this moment of happiness with Sally.

(Bartley hums a bit of the tune being played.)

B: People are laughing and spinning around!

A: How long have you known Sally?

B: All my life. She loves me. (Alice moves Bartley to the next significant scene.) We're up in the barn and we're kissing. I'm touching her, and we just love each other very much. He [George's father] catches us.

A: Are you clothed, the two of you?

B: Halfway. We pull things. He gets really angry. He's yelling at me and I'm yelling at him. I'm saying, how dare he, that I'm old enough to have my own life. Sally is crying. I'm a little bigger [than him] but we're pretty much the same size. He orders me to go home. I leave and walk down. (Bartley becomes distressed.)

A: Are you all right?

B: (crying) He rapes Sally. (Bartley sobs and Alice comforts her, then asks her to probe further into the events in George's life. She sees George back at home in the cabin.) He walks back in. He's smiling, he's smirking. I lunge at him.

A: Do you know what he's done?

B: I don't know how I would know, [but] I know for some reason.

A: There might be some way that you found this out.

B: (speaking rapidly) He's laughing. I lunge at him and I hit him with my fist, and then I strangle him. He pushes me away. He's just as strong as I am. We're fighting.

A: Does anybody get hurt?

B: No. My mom comes in and stops it.

(Alice asks Bartley to let go of George's life, and to search her Higher Self for the lifetime in which the hatred first took root. Alice surmises that the incarnations as George and Joyce were consecutive, and that their premature deaths by murder had a common cause. Bartley moves again through time and finds herself a strapping, blond young man of about eighteen in Rome. He has command of a chariot drawn by a single white horse, and he is awaiting the start of a race. The race begins, and the horses thunder down the course. The young man is high on adrenaline and wants to win. Then something unexpected—and tragic—happens. His chariot swerves and hits a chariot abreast of him. The other driver loses his balance and is knocked from the chariot. He dies instantly when his head is crushed by the wheels of the blond youth's chariot. The shock to Bartley is overwhelming, especially when she realizes that the dead driver was her brother in that life. She is instantly filled with remorse and guilt. She moves to other earlier scenes of that life in which they share drinks and laughter and the company of young women, and one in which Bartley, as the Roman charioteer, lies sick in bed while his brother tends him. The bond between the two brothers is intense, full of admiration and love. After these glimpses, Alice asks Bartley to let go of this life.)

A: I would like to move you up to your own higher mind. You might look at these relationships that you had with Roger in the past and analyze how they relate to the present time. How does [the life as Joyce] relate to the present?

B: It's the same verbal abuse, not as much physical abuse. He has strangled me before, once so badly I thought I was going to die.

A: What about the life in which you were George and he was your father?

B: That was more of a very cold relationship, with more distance, not as much physical violence. We had a lot of hate.

A: What about the relationship in Rome in which he was your brother?

B: We had a good relationship, we loved each other.

A: I'd like you to look at that life in Rome and be able to forgive yourself for that accident. It was not your fault.

B: But it doesn't matter that it wasn't my fault!

A: Why?

B: (crying) Just the fact that he was gone. I missed him.

A: It's important for you to be able to forgive yourself, to let go of that baggage. You don't need to carry it around any longer. If you've carried that guilt with you so long and into so many other lifetimes, it might be that you are feeling that you deserve the violence. You feel you did this terrible thing to him and you bring this guilt forward into other lives and you allow yourself to be abused. You allowed yourself to be murdered in two of these lives. It's time to let go of that guilt. Do you think you can look back on that life in Rome and truly forgive yourself for what happened?

B: (crying) I think so. I forgive myself for that (unconvincingly).

A: I'd like you to make me believe you.

B: (emphatically) I do forgive myself.

A: If that's truly the karmic cause for these two murders in these previous lives, that's a very big price to pay for an accident. You have more than paid for it now.

B: I don't understand why, if my brother forgave

me for an accident, why he would come back in every life and murder me.

A: There might be some other lives involved as well. It is time for you to let go of that guilt, and to be treated with the love, respect, and dignity that you deserve.

(Alice then has Bartley forgive the previous incarnations of Roger, as Joyce's husband and George's father. Bartley lets go of the anger and hate she experienced. She knows the violence must stop.)

A: Great wisdom can come out of this for you. It is up to you to change yourself.

(Because the regression has been traumatic for Bartley, Alice believes she could benefit by looking into the future in a progression. She needs to see the positive effects of change, and realize that a loving, happy relationship is possible for her. At first, Bartley is uncertain. The idea of looking into her future is a little frightening, but she has felt safe and guided throughout the regression and so agrees. Alice takes her ahead in time. The scenes are misty, not as clearly defined as those from the past. Bartley experiences a dramatic shift in emotion. She sees herself married to a tall Englishman with curly blond hair named Peter, who works in the creative arts. She observes herself and Peter enjoying a vacation. She stands overlooking the Grand Canyon at sunrise as he drives up in a car. She experiences a tender moment of intimacy shortly after the birth of their baby daughter. In this progression, Bartley is no longer at her present job, and is living somewhere other than New York. Words float into her head: *Perfect. Fine. Wonderful.* She guesses this vision takes place in 1989. She returns to full consciousness.)

Later, as Bartley went over and over the regression in her mind, she was awed by the power and intensity of the experience. Everything she had witnessed had been vivid and tangible. Most incredible of all were the emotions she'd felt. "I've never felt such emotional pain, or been so emotionally high in love," she thought.

The past-life regression and future-life progression proved to be catalysts for far-reaching transformation for Bartley. She felt liberated of the oppressive energies weighing down her life. She went through a period of rapid growth and change, during which she began to feel spiritually centered. She was able to let go of Roger and put the relationship behind her. She felt like a new person.

Bartley embarked on an exploration of other past lives in further regressions. She discovered that her long-time affinity for England stemmed from a series of at least six lives there. Her present work in advertising took her often to England. Now she knew why she had always felt at home there.

Several months after her first session with Alice, Bartley entered the elevator in her apartment building one evening. Inside was a tall blond man whom she recognized, though she knew she had never met him before. "Your name is Peter," she thought, her pulse quickening in anticipation.

The man looked down at her and smiled. "Hello, my name is Peter," he said in an English accent. "What's yours?"

"I can't believe it!" thought Bartley. She remembered the warm, wonderful feelings she had enjoyed in the progression. She had half believed the vision, half not. Was this the man who would make it come true? Bartley grew even more hopeful when, during their short conversation, she discovered that Peter was a writer. Everything—his name, height, hair, occupation, and heritage—fit the progression exactly.

Peter took Bartley's telephone number but did not

give her his. It was unlisted, he explained. He promised to call. By the time Bartley left for a trip to England two days later, he had not made good on the promise. Nor did he call after she returned to New York two weeks later. Bartley would have shrugged it off as another of the vagaries of single life, had it not been for the progression. She manufactured a tale to obtain his unlisted number from the telephone company operator and called him. No, no, he hadn't forgotten her, he assured her; how about lunch?

Bartley's fragile bubble of hope burst on the lunch date. Peter was not at all what she was looking for; in fact, he reminded her of Roger in some ways. He admitted he was living with a woman, whom he was more than willing to deceive by seeing Bartley on the sly. Bartley saw immediately where that would lead: to more pain for herself. She didn't want any part of it and decided not to see him again.

"What is going on here?" she wondered afterward. "I thought I was through with men who'll hurt me!" She was devastated by the unexpected turn of events. Doubts lingered in her mind. Was she giving up that marvelous, happy future? She resolved to work through her feelings and discover why she had met Peter. After a great deal of meditation, she found the answer. She had been given a lesson in making choices. She had arrived at a crossroads. Peter represented the old path to yet another unhappy experience. Before her lay a new path. If she took it, she was certain she would find happiness.

Bartley continued to grow spiritually through study and meditation. She had relationships with men, but none of them caught fire. One day in 1986, she consulted a well-known trance channeler in Manhattan. The channeler told Bartley that she had a soul mate on the planet, but she wouldn't be with him until May

1987. He had blond, curly hair and worked in the creative arts. The elusive mystery man again!

In May 1987, Bartley went to London. For three years, she had been working a great deal with an English photographer named William, who aspired to be a film writer and director. They were good friends but not romantically involved. He had wavy blond hair, which he wore short. But when Bartley saw him that May, he had let his hair grow, and the waves were now curly.

One evening, Bartley and William went out to dinner. Both had recently broken off romances. All of a sudden, they seemed to see each other in a new way. It was electrifying, and Bartley knew immediately that *this was it*.

Events in Bartley's life then moved swiftly, as though directed by unseen forces. Within months, she lost her job at the New York agency. Her apartment building became a co-op and she had to move. She did: to London. She left the advertising agency world and went to work as a stylist, finding props for commercials and still photography. In June 1988, Bartley and William were married. *Perfect. Fine. Wonderful*. The progression will be completely fulfilled when a baby arrives, and Bartley is certain there is one somewhere in the future.

She surmised that she got the name "Peter" in the progression because her meeting with Peter was on the horizon. Did she really see the future, or was the progression a fantasy that then materialized to her through her own desire? Perhaps it was a little of both.

Bartley's journey through her past lives led to inner changes that left her feeling like a new person. She had learned both the law of karma and the law of grace. Her overwhelming sense of guilt had caused her to allow herself to become a victim of violence again and again. In order to break the cycle and grow spiritually, she had to first forgive herself for taking a life, then forgive Roger, the soul who was her brother in that Roman life, who had allowed resentment over the tragedy to fester into hate and revenge in subsequent lives. It wasn't easy, but it was literally a matter of life and death.

CHAPTER TEN

Phobias and Physical Karma

In Sanskrit, they're called *samskaras:* subtle impressions, or imprints, carried over from one life to another, which manifest themselves in physical appearance and personality traits. At death, according to the Hindus, the soul passes into its subtle body or astral body, which retains all of these impressions and carries them into the next physical body. A similar concept in Buddhism is *skandhas* ("heaps" or "aggregates"), remnants of the personality, including physical form, perceptions, feelings, impulses, and personal consciousness, which survive death and are reincarnated in a new personality.

Phobias and physical traits are among the *samskaras* that are troublesome and debilitating. Many people have phobias that cannot be attributed to traumatic events in their present lives. How does one account, for example, for a fear of horses when one has seldom been near horses? The answer may lie in past-life traumas.

In his research on spontaneous past-life recall

among children, Ian Stevenson found a high incidence of phobias related to the mode of death of the previous personality, especially when the death was violent or involved prolonged or great suffering. Among 252 instances involving violent death, 127, or fully half, engendered phobias in the reincarnated personality. One of the most unusual cases is that of Ravi Shankar, a Hindu boy born in 1951 (not to be confused with the musician of the same name), six months after Munna Ashokumar, a six-year-old who lived near Shankar's family, was savagely murdered. Little Munna's throat had been slit and his head nearly severed, apparently by a barber and a washerman. The men were arrested and one confessed, but he retracted his confession. They were released due to lack of evidence, and the crime went unpunished.

Ravi Shankar was born with a startling birthmark: a long, jagged line slashed across his throat. It varied from about an eighth to a quarter of an inch in width, and was dark and stippled, much like scar tissue from a healed knife wound. When Ravi Shankar reached the age of two or three, he began to talk spontaneously about "his" murder. He named his murderers and described the murder site, and painted a rich picture of his life as Munna. He also had strong phobias toward razors, barbers, and washermen. He said he wanted to avenge his own murder. Munna's father wanted to avenge the murder, too. When he heard about Ravi Shankar and verified to his satisfaction that he was Munna reincarnated, he sought to reopen the case against the accused men based on evidence provided by Ravi Shankar's past-life memories. Not surprisingly, the courts wouldn't hear of it.

Curiously, the ragged birthmark began moving up Ravi Shankar's throat. By 1964, it was under the ridge of the chin and had shortened to about two inches in length. At that time, he no longer was afraid of one of the accused murderers and no longer recognized the second. By 1969, the mark had moved up farther under the chin, near the chin's point. Ravi Shankar was then eighteen and a student in college. He had lost all the memories of Munna's life and death, and no longer harbored a desire for revenge. He had gotten over his fears of razors, barbers, and washermen. No satisfactory explanation has ever been given for the movement of the birthmark.

Other death-related phobias are tied to places, such as bridges and cliffs, or to foods, in cases related to poisonings.

In many of these cases involving children, the phobia diminishes or disappears with the passage of time, as do the past-life memories themselves, as happened to Ravi Shankar. Some phobias remain lifelong.

People who undergo past-life regression often discover that their present phobias have past-life causes, and that most are related to death and severe trauma. Many subjects are surprised to find that their phobias disappear after the discovery of the root cause. We don't know why this happens; perhaps the process of examining past lives releases beneficial or healing energy that alleviates the problem. The results are often so swift—sometimes occurring after a single regression session—that many people seek past-life regression solely to try to cure themselves of phobias interfering with their lives. Sometimes past-life regression works when other methods have failed.

Alice T., the Manhattan past-life regressionist mentioned earlier, has done a great deal of work with clients who have phobias. Two clients once shared a similar phobia, but with unusual causes. Alice T. related one case:

A woman came to me with a terrible fear of injections, having blood drawn, or having any kind of invasive medical procedure, whether she herself was experiencing it or merely witnessing it. Her phobia was so profound that it would cause her to faint. In fact, the day before our session, she had passed out while attending a circumcision.

The cause of her phobia was twofold: her present-life birth experience, which was by cesarean section, and an earlier incarnation somewhere in Central or South America, in which she was a woman whose infant was to be sacrificed in a ritual. It was considered an honor in that society to have one's child chosen. But I would imagine that even in such a culture, it's not easy for a mother to sacrifice a child. In her case, the sacrifice was done by fire. The baby was put into a fire, but it didn't die right away and was in a lot of pain. The suffering of her infant horrified her, and she felt compelled to end its suffering. So she grabbed the first thing she could find, which was a tool or weapon with a blade, and killed her baby so that it would not suffer through the burning.

The soul who was her baby in that life is her mother in her present life. During birth, the soul is sometimes in the fetus and sometimes out of it. She was out of the fetus and observed her mother being cut open. She associated her mother's surgery with the sacrifice, and believed that she was once again causing this soul, whom she loved dearly, excruciating pain. This caused her tremendous grief and guilt, which in turn caused her phobia.

About two weeks after our session, she had to go to the doctor's to have blood drawn. For the first time in at least six years, she didn't pass out.

Lynn L. of Manhattan explained her similar phobia:

I had severe anxiety whenever I was given an injection. Even the prospect of an injection or surgery prompted anxiety. I would hyperventilate, want to cry, break out in a cold sweat, get nauseated, and, less frequently, vomit. If I so much as saw a surgical procedure on TV, I would begin to experience the phobic symptoms and have to turn off the program. A couple of times I had minor surgery that usually was performed on an outpatient basis, yet I had to stay overnight in the hospital and have a general anesthetic, so that I would be totally unconscious during the experience.

In an earlier lifetime in Africa, I was a woman who was pregnant, but not by my husband; I had been unfaithful. To punish me, the villagers tied me to a stake and slashed my stomach open. I died and my baby died. When I was born by cesarean section in this life, I viewed the birth. I remembered the degradation and humiliation I'd experienced in the African life, and, as I witnessed my mother being cut open, I perceived her suffering degradation and humiliation and thought I was the cause. Once I discovered the cause of this phobia, I was able to release it. Now I don't think I'm any more squeamish than the average person.

For Laurie McQuary, the psychic consultant in Portland, Oregon, her fears of death by fire and drowning have roots in her own past lives. The information was revealed to her in past-life dreams, which she described:

One dream opened with me walking down cobblestone streets that turned into dusty roads. I was walking amidst a group of people, dressed in a burlap or rough material that was either creamy colored or white. I had long red hair down to my waist. I had this sense of calm, that these people were protecting me and taking me someplace and I would be fine. All of a sudden, off to my right was a house. It was more like a cottage, very simple. The group of people was trying to get me to go into the cottage to exchange identities with another person who was going to take my place. They were trying to protect me from wherever I was going. I wouldn't change. I said, "No, I have to go where I'm going."

They continued with me, and I ended up at a fire pit that was probably a good five or six feet deep. I was thrown into the pit and fire was thrown on top of me. The most amazing thing was that as I lay in the pit, I could see the fire above me. I couldn't have crawled out of it easily at all. As the fire was falling toward me, I had such a sense of calm. I said, "I'm going to die, and I'm fine." When I woke from that dream, I knew I had died for being a witch in a past life. I feel it might have been in Ireland or Scotland. It felt like a very long time ago—it might even have been in ancient Druid times.

I have a fear of drowning, especially in anything covered like a car. I had a dream that I was on a floating planklike object in a huge river. I could see across the river and see other people clinging to planklike pieces. As I passed this one group, I thought, "That's my mother, though it's not the mother that I have in this lifetime." In the dream I said to myself, "This is part of the reason I'm so afraid of drowning.'' I knew I had lost my mother in that lifetime through drowning.

PHYSICAL KARMA

Edgar Cayce was twenty-one in 1898 when his remarkable ability to give medical diagnoses by clairvoyance was discovered. He suffered laryngitis and had lost his voice. No amount of medical treatment helped, and he was forced to give up his job as a salesman. A traveling hypnotist who came to Cayce's Kentucky town was able to hypnotize Cayce and improve his voice during trance, but posthypnotic suggestion failed to work. Cayce's condition caught the attention of another man, Al Layne, who hypnotized Cayce and asked him to describe the nature of his affliction and a cure. The hypnotized Cayce said his condition was partial paralysis of the inferior muscle of the vocal cords, caused by nerve strain, and that increasing the circulation to the vocal cords would relieve the condition. Layne gave that suggestion, and then watched Cayce's neck turn bright red as blood circulation increased for about twenty minutes. When Cayce awoke, he had his voice back. Layne suggested that Cayce try to diagnose others while in trance. Cayce was dubious, yet his success was astounding.

When word of his ability spread, thousands of suffering people began contacting Cayce for help. Over the course of his life, Cayce gave more than 25,000 physical readings. He knew nothing of medicine, yet he was able to describe in medical terms the nature of a person's affliction and give instructions to alleviate the symptoms or cure them. To give a reading, he simply lay down and relaxed. The client did not have to be present; Cayce could give readings long distance, for someone anywhere in the world.

Cayce began giving medical diagnoses in 1901. He

first alluded to reincarnation in 1923, and from then on many of his physical readings involved past lives. He often attributed the cause of a physical problem to past-life actions and told the client he or she was experiencing the effects of karma. Not all conditions were karmic, and of those that were, he was frank in stating whether or not they could be cured. Some could not be cured, but could be alleviated. He repeatedly emphasized that the health of the body depends on the health of the mind and spirit, and that ill health cannot be cured without being preceded by a change in attitude.

The body, the mind, the soul are one within the physical forces; for the body is indeed the temple of the living God. In each entity there is that portion which is a part of the Universal Force, and is that which lives on. All must coordinate and cooperate.

—Edgar Cayce, Reading 1593-1

But remember, mind is the builder. . . . Don't look to material things—look for the spiritual. Plan what you will do for others, and what you will do with the healing grace that may be manifested in the body-forces through the power within and the prayer to the Christ within the self.

—Reading 3681-1

The effect that the mind and emotions can have on health is ancient knowledge and has been the basis of many healing systems, like the 5,000-year-old Ayurvedic system of India. In the West, mind and body became separated in medicine and science. Only recently have efforts been made by some in the medical establishment to reunite them in the field of behavioral medicine, which takes into account both mind

153

and body in illness and disease. From the standpoint of reincarnation, there is an added incentive to purge negative emotions from one's life, for in addition to affecting health in the present, they may affect health in the future as well.

According to the Cayce readings, the cause and effect working of karma is not necessarily literal, nor does it always occur immediately in the next life. Cayce was sometimes asked by clients why karmic debts had skipped lives. His answer was simple: "Because it [karma] was unable to [act] before."

One of the most important points to be drawn from the Cayce readings is that *attitude* and *intent* can create physical karma; here he echoes the Eastern teachings that karma is created by thought and motivation. The paybacks for mockery, scorn, hate, jealousy, and indifference may take the form of physical deformity, debilitating illness, loss of limb or bodily function in accidents, or degenerative diseases. A number of Cayce's clients were told that their problems stemmed from lives in Rome, when they participated in the persecution of Christians by mocking and scorning them or gleefully watching them torn apart by lions in the Coliseum. Such persons in their present lives suffered from polio, tuberculosis of the hip, lameness, and similar afflictions. The readings emphasize that tacit approval of cruelty and abuse also incurs negative karma.

Tacit approval also may be experienced collectively, as in a group, race, or nation that tolerates violence to others. Given that, we may expect to see many karmic scores settled not only with those who actively helped the Nazis massacre Jews and other innocents, but with the millions who stood by and allowed this to happen.

Some karmic effects seem to manifest themselves in unusual ways. For example, Cayce said that one young boy who was anemic had lived in Persia, where he had caused great bloodshed; hence in the present, his own blood had been robbed of its vitality.

Cayce's examples serve to remind us that it is not just our deeds that speed or inhibit our spiritual growth, but our words, thoughts, and emotions, as well. As Cayce said:

For, as given of old, each soul shall give an account of every idle word spoken. It shall pay every whit.

—Reading 3124-1

PAST-LIFE REGRESSION AND PHYSICAL KARMA

Many of Cayce's recommended treatments were elaborate, and, depending on the problem, improvement was sometimes slight or gradual. More recently, past-life regressionists have helped others to alleviate or cure *some types* of physical problems by finding the past life involved and facilitating a release of negative energy. It is not understood exactly how or why this process works, but, as for phobias, it is in *some cases* very effective.

Obesity, for example, is often found to be related to either starvation or sexual abuse in previous lives. The individual in this life overeats to prevent starvation again, or to make the body undesirable and therefore prevent further sexual abuse. In addition, Cayce attributed obesity to neglect and abuse of the body in a previous life. Making these past-life connections seems to resolve the matter on some level of consciousness, and the individual often is able to marshal the resolve to shed the unwanted pounds.

Past-life regression has been found to help alleviate some chronic physical complaints, such as headaches and back pain. Here again, it must be understood that past-life regression is no magic bullet and is not a substitute for medical treatment. Nevertheless, relief has been attained in cases where traditional medicine has been unable to diagnose the cause of the problem or treat it successfully. Said Laurie McQuary:

Medical conditions come through often in a past-life reading. Once someone with a terrible pain in his side came to see me. He'd been to doctor after doctor but could never get a diagnosis. Fortunately, he is metaphysically oriented, and he figured it was psychically tied to a past life.

We narrowed it down to something that was cyclical in nature and revolved around a friend of his in the present. Whenever he spent a lot of time with this person, he would get a stabbing pain in his side. They were friends from childhood, but the friend was irresponsible and had a lot of problems. This man, on the other hand, was very responsible, and was always trying to counsel his friend and help him out.

In a past life, they had been two monks, standing out in a garden and arguing. The one who is the friend now was in that lifetime very unhappy as a monk and wanted out. He was always questioning his faith. My client was always trying to counsel him. Suddenly this friend picked up a sharp stick or hoe and struck him in the side in anger, and it killed him.

It seemed that in the present, whenever my client argued with his friend, he relived the moment when the friend lost control and killed him in that other life. From the time we discovered this on, the man's pain started to diminish, and it was gone within two months.

I send a lot of people who have medical conditions that may be tied to past lives to a hypnotherapist [Sam McMains of Portland]. One was a woman who suffered chest pain. The doctors could find nothing. She was absolutely opposed to the idea of reincarnation, yet she knew she had to do something. Sam regressed her. She saw herself as a slave in the United States, standing on a slave block. She couldn't understand a word that anyone was saying around her, because she had just come from Africa. She was hauled off the block and put in chains. She tripped and a wagon ran over her and crushed her chest. She came out of that regression remembering everything, and was totally convinced about reincarnation. Her pain went away.

Sandee Mac, the Houston hypnotherapist, related:

Sometimes physical problems relate to more than one past life. One woman I worked with had chronic colon problems, a lot of pain and blockage. The condition was tied in with more than one past life, including one in which she was stabbed in the colon area. Another woman came to me because she had suddenly developed a fear of flying. She had flown extensively throughout her life without a problem, until she took her first trip to Europe. The fear was activated when she was coming home and flying over the water. In regression, we found that in World War II, she was a soldier in a military plane that was hit and went down over the water. I asked her unconscious if there was another lifetime involved and got the answer, yes, in another life she had drowned in a shipwreck.

THE HANGMAN'S HEADACHES

Past-life regression helped Pat, a New York woman, to recover from severe and chronic headaches:

I went back to a life in England where I victimized others. The first thing I saw was a great castle with a moat. My first thought was that I was the queen or princess of the castle. As soon as the thought materialized, I instantly found myself on the other side of the castle. Then I realized that I was the hangman! I saw a scaffold. I began to see a lot of pictures of people, old people, young people, men, women, and I knew that they were people I had hung. I don't know what century it was. I had the feeling there were political difficulties, a time of great strife, and many people were being hung.

I felt a great deal of emotion, of horror—how could that be me, this mild-mannered, *nice* person who chases a roach out of her apartment rather than kill it? I was horrified that I had taken part in such violence!

That was all that I saw about that lifetime. I was able to get a sense of who I was as a man. I was between the ages of thirty and fifty, and was not educated or capable of doing much else. I was emotionally frail, but I had no conscious moral conflict about what I was doing. It was my job, I did it and I did it well. I didn't see a picture of myself, but I got a sense of my appearance. I was about five-foot-ten with reddish-brown hair and a slight build.

Seeing this life enabled me to get over chronic headaches. When I was about nineteen, I began to suffer from headaches that started with a pain in my neck and worked their way up. They got progressively worse over the years. Sometimes they were debilitating, forcing me to go to bed. I had various medical tests, including a CAT scan, because my doctor thought I might have a brain tumor. I didn't. I tried acupuncture but received only temporary relief. Finally, after regressing to the life in England, I stopped having those headaches. They were a product of guilt. Once I was able to view the life and look at it closely, the guilt was released.

The regression also stimulated a desire in Pat to visit England, a country previously of little interest to her—perhaps for past-life reasons—despite her enjoyment of travel. Within a few months of the regression, she planned her trip. While browsing through travel folders, she was startled to see a picture of the very castle she had seen in her regression: Warwick castle on the Avon River near Stratford-on-Avon. Warwick, one of the finest medieval fortresses in all of Europe, housed a dungeon where many people had been tortured for various crimes throughout the years. The water that Pat had thought was the castle's moat was the Avon River. She visited the castle during her stay in England.

A few years later, Pat discovered that the hangman's life was connected to her most recent past life. As the hangman, she had given her tacit approval to the executions, which created a karmic debt.

I was a Jewish girl who was killed in a Nazi concentration camp, Dachau, I believe, in the early 1940s. I was only about five or six.

I have gotten information on this life from five different sources. The first as an intuitive flash, a picture of a Nazi officer in a woolen uniform coat as seen from behind. All I could see was the right lower quadrant of his coat, although I knew what the front looked like. The second source was a channel who told me my most recent life was as a concentration camp victim in World War II. The third source was a friend who was regressed to a life where he knew me in that World War II life. The fourth source was my own regression to that life by a colleague. The fifth was my astrologer, who said my chart showed that in my last life I'd died violently as a child.

For me, this seems to be the perfect karmic balance. In the life in England, I hanged people I didn't know or have any personal vendetta against. I was simply doing my job, following orders. In the life in World War II, the people who killed me had no personal vendetta against me—they were just doing their job.

THE CASTRATED ROMAN

Physical karma from a victim's trauma also occurs in this account from Barbara Hand Clow of Santa Fe.

Three or four years before I had my first past-life regression, I began to develop a cyst in my neck. It was about the size of a pea or bean and felt like it was in one of the neck glands. I was very fearful that it was cancer, even though I have always felt that I would never get cancer in this life. I did not go to the doctor.

The cause of the cyst was revealed when I began past-life regression with Gregory Paxson in Chicago. I relived part of a past life in which I was a Roman man, small in stature and about twenty-one or twenty-two years in age. I was taken to a prison, but instead of being put in a cell, the soldiers took me into a room and forced me to lie on a wooden table. A man in a white tunic came in and castrated me with a thin, razor-sharp knife. The pain and terror were incredible, and I saw myself witnessing my mutilation from outside my body. It was horrible.

As Greg and I went over the incident, I noticed that I had a sharp pain in my neck. Greg said, "Go to that part of your body and find out what's going on." I then saw that one of the soldiers was holding a small knife right next to my neck, cutting my neck as they were castrating me. If I struggled to rise off the table and get away, he cut into my neck. Reliving this incident enabled me to release negative energy in my emotional body, which in turn was affecting me physically. Three weeks later, the cyst went away and never returned.

STABBED BY A JILTED SUITOR

Annie B.'s experience with a karmic physical condition was triggered when the man who created her problem in the past reappeared in her present life:

I woke up one morning with a pain in my chest that wouldn't go away. I went to a doctor but he couldn't find anything wrong. After about three months of pain, someone suggested I look into past lives. I was skeptical, but gave it a try. I was regressed, and immediately saw a side of a building and some bushes. It seemed to be in Italy in about the 1300s. There were three persons besides myself. Two of the others were a man I was refusing to marry and my mother in that life, who wanted me to marry this man. The man was stabbing me in the chest because I wouldn't marry him. I could feel the knife going in, right in the same place where I was having the pain. He killed me.

I realized that the man who stabbed me was now a man I'd recently started dating. I didn't like him very much, though I was strongly attracted to him physically. I realized that the pain had begun several weeks after meeting him. It must have been triggered by the past-life connection. After I saw the past life, the pain healed by itself. I guess there is such a thing as old psychic wounds.

The experience also helped Annie see that she was dating this man for the wrong reasons. She broke off the relationship.

RAPED AND HANGED

Alexandria (a pseudonym) lives in Connecticut and works as a hair designer. Her co-workers and customers see her as an attractive young woman with an abundance of energy and enthusiasm, who always thinks of others first. Privately, Alexandria has struggled with physical discomfort, depression, and problems in her relationships, the solutions to which seemed to elude her. Past-life regression gave her a new perspective, and insights that surprised her. Here is Alexandria's account of her experience:

There were three main reasons I decided to have a past-life regression. About five years ago, I started doing yoga and a lot of things got stirred up. I began to feel a lot of tension, a tightness, in my groin. I noticed it a lot when I was driving, like I was holding a ball between my legs. It was a very uncomfortable feeling.

Secondly, I felt unhappy. It was a vague unhappiness, around me all the time. I could be anywhere, like at a party, and be outwardly happy but unhappy on the inside, like I didn't know where I belonged. It was weird.

Finally, I felt stuck in a pattern of bad relationships that invariably involved alcohol or substance abuse. My father was an alcoholic, and the men who came into my life also had problems with alcohol or drugs. I always questioned the abuse or put it down or tried to stop it. I also did that with my father before he died. It seemed like a chain, a progression of events, and I wanted to break it. I tried group therapy for a while, but that issue was never resolved. Then I did est[1], which made me more aware of the pattern I was in. A friend recommended past-life regression, and I thought perhaps it would help me let go of the tightness in my groin, and discover why I was unhappy and stuck in a pattern of bad relationships.

I was raised Catholic and didn't believe in reincarnation until I started the yoga. The first yoga book I read was [Jess Stearn's] *Yoga, Youth, and Reincarnation*. I also read Edgar Cayce. I was attracted to the whole Eastern philosophy of eternal oneness and eternal spirit, and the idea of coming back to resolve things until we get everything right.

Alexandria's past-life regression was done under light hypnosis. She asked to see lives that would help her to understand her three problems.

---

[1] est: initials for Erhard Seminars Training, a system of experiential philosophy developed in the 1960s by Werner Erhard (real name John Paul Rosenberg), a former auto dealer and trainer of encyclopedia salesmen.

The first thing I saw was that I was in a cabin. There was a fire going in the fireplace—I could hear it crackling. I was alone. I was in my early thirties, about the same age I am now. I was wearing a long blue dress.

I heard Indians outside. They attacked the cabin and broke in. There were about a half a dozen of them. They dragged me out and put me on a horse. The next thing I saw was that I was somewhere in a forest and was tied up on the ground. The Indian [braves] raped me. I was very frightened—I was afraid they were going to kill me. They eventually did, but I don't know how. I didn't go through the death. I don't recall that I tried to defend myself.

Then I moved on to another experience. I got a very clear picture of it. I was sitting at a dark and heavy table in my house with my younger sister. I had been reading. I had glasses and gray hair that I wore tied back. I had a long dress on. I got the feeling that it was sometime around the seventeenth century, but I don't know where. There was a village.

My sister had come over to warn me that the town men were after us because we were supposedly witches. We were healers and they didn't understand about healers. We ran away with other women who were also healers. My sister had her child, a girl, with her. I don't remember any other children. We ran into a cave and huddled together. My sister's child fell and needed some kind of root or leaf, a medicinal plant. I said I would get it. I went outside, and the townspeople caught me. They took me out somewhere and raped me and broke my back—I've always had back pain—and they hanged me from a gallows.

I felt very sad because I couldn't get back to

my sister and help her child. She is my sister in the present life, a year older than me.

Afterward, I understood why I had the tightness, and I was able to let go of it. I also felt I was on a different plane with my sister the next time I spoke to her. I saw her relationship with her daughter differently. Before I was judgmental about how she was raising her child; now I give her credit for being the loving mother that she is. I felt moved by that. She's always loved and adored me, and I never felt worth it. Seeing this relationship in a new light was unexpected.

I didn't get to work on why I'm in a pattern of bad relationships, but I did get something else out of the witch life. The men hunted witches and had no understanding of me. That's like the same thing now. The men I get involved with have no understanding of who I am. It also has to do with me not communicating, and I am going to have to work on that.

The sadness lifted and now I feel great. I'm much more confident in my work. I still have back pain, but not as often, and it occurs only when I'm under very great stress. I can release it on my own. I'm happy and I truly believe that the universe will support me if I go with the flow.

Sometimes the physical karma left by a past life is a birthmark or a birth defect. Birthmarks, in fact, are the most universally reported characteristic in all reported reincarnation cases. Ravi Shankar, mentioned earlier, had a birthmark around his neck where his previous personality had suffered his death wound. Another unusual birth defect case recorded in Ian Stevenson's research is H. A. Wijeratne, who was born in 1947 in Uggalkaltota, Sri Lanka (then known as Ceylon), with a pronounced deformity of his right breast and arm. His parents attributed it to an unknown past-life karma. As the boy grew older, he began to remind the father of his younger brother. The child was dark-complected and distinctly different from the other, fairer children in the family. At age two and a half, the boy began to talk about murdering his wife in his previous life; that was why he had been born deformed. The father's younger brother had been executed in 1928 for murdering his wife.

OFF WITH HIS HEAD!

Andorian, a young man who lives in the Southwest, has a birthmark similar to the one Ravi Shankar had at birth:

I have a very large birthmark around my neck. It's a reddish, jagged line that circles my neck at about the collar line. I believe it comes from a past life in which I had my head chopped off. It was a life I spent with my present ex-wife in a Middle Eastern country, about A.D. 600. I worked as a palace architect. I was well educated and lived very comfortably. I designed our home for my wife and three children, two boys and a girl. It was pretty elaborate, with a swimming pool, big rooms, and long silk curtains. We had servants.

A man framed me for stealing one of the palace objects—it was a vase with a lot of gold decoration. This other man was very deceptive and manipulative, while I was straightforward and believed the truth would take care of itself. I think he was the one who really stole the vase. He convinced the king that no one else but me could have done it, because I had a lot of power and access throughout the palace. I was sent off to jail and sentenced to be executed. The king felt that he had treated me like a son and I had stabbed him in the back. The execution took place in the throne room, because it was his pleasure to see me being executed. I knelt over a stone block and the executioner cut off my head with a mammoth, crescent-shaped sword. I wasn't so much afraid of dying as I was of my family being scarred by shame.

I'd hidden all our money and told my wife where it was before I was killed. Afterward, she grabbed the money and took herself and the children far away to start a new life under a new name. It was hard for her; I don't think I was supposed to die like that in that life. She was a lot younger than me, and she had to learn how to adapt and cope without me. The oldest child was seven and the youngest was three when I was killed.

The birthmark hasn't caused me any problems. I think I was able to accept what happened to me at the time, and not go out angry.

CHAPTER ELEVEN

Skills and Talents

Samskaras also take the form of skills, talents, and inclinations toward certain professions and occupations. Those who are at the tops of their chosen fields perhaps have honed their skills and paid their dues many, many times over.

Some believe that reincarnation and the law of attraction (soul connections that are not apparent on the surface)—not heredity or environment, or a combination of the two—are responsible for geniuses and child prodigies. Mozart, then, was not a miracle, but one who had served a musical apprenticeship over a series of lives, building his talent and skills until he achieved vast creativity and knowledge.

Ralph Waldo Emerson alluded to genius as a product of reincarnation in "Representative Men," his essay on Emanuel Swedenborg, the Swedish mystic of the eighteenth century. The reason for the "intuition of genius," Emerson said, "would lead us into that property which Plato denoted as reminiscence and which is implied by the Brahmins in the tenet of Transmigration.''

According to Ian Stevenson, no empirical studies of regression cases provide sufficient evidence to support reincarnation as an explanation for child prodigies. No known child prodigies of the West have claimed to derive their skills from previous lives, though a few in Asia have done so. Stevenson believes that the musical gifts of Mozart, Beethoven, Brahms, and Bach, for example, most likely were due to the combined influence by heredity and early environment. All of these composers had musician fathers and were reared in a musical environment.

But Stevenson does not dismiss reincarnation as a possibility, pointing out that numerous examples exist of exceptional talent and unusual abilities that cannot be attributed to heredity and environment. George Frideric Handel (1685–1759), for example, developed his musical talent despite a lack of interest and even opposition on the part of his family. Likewise, Florence Nightingale (1820–1910), the English nurse who founded modern nursing, and Elizabeth Fry (1780–1845), the English Quaker who achieved major reforms in the English prison system, also received no support from their families. Still other highly talented individuals do receive family encouragement for their ambitions, but exhibit them in such a remarkable way at such a young age that reincarnation seems to be the only plausible explanation.

Take the case of Jean-François Champollion (1790–1832), who announced his intention to decipher Egyptian hieroglyphics before he was twelve years old. He was trained in archaeology by his older brother, Jean Jacques Champollion-Figeac, and succeeded in deciphering the Rosetta Stone in 1821. Similarly, Heinrich Schliemann (1822–90) displayed an unusual passion for the writings of Homer as a child, and was not yet eight when he said he would discover the ruins of Troy. He went on to earn a fortune in business, and retired at age forty-one to search for Homeric sites. He not only unearthed Troy but also made significant archaeological finds at Mycenae, Ithaca, and Tiryns.

UNLEARNED LANGUAGES

One of the most exceptional skills linked to past lives is that of *xenoglossy,* or the ability to speak in an unlearned tongue. To past-life researchers, xenoglossy provides some of the strongest evidence for survival, and therefore possibly for reincarnation, for language cannot be transferred by telepathy; it must be learned. Cases of authentic xenoglossy are rare. "Recitative xenoglossy" is the recitation of an unlearned language with neither comprehension nor the ability to converse. "Responsive xenoglossy" is the ability to converse in an unknown language. When xenoglossy occurs, it usually does so in hypnotic regression in a fragmented, recitative fashion. In most cases, there is a high degree of inaccuracy, which makes it difficult to prove that the individual did not pick up the phrases at some point in a lifetime of reading or learning.

There are, however, some cases of responsive xenoglossy that seem to have no natural explanation. In 1862, a mesmerist named Prince Galitzin hypnotized an uneducated German woman who began speaking fluent French, a language she did not know. She said she had lived in eighteenth-century France as a woman and had murdered her husband, and now was being punished with a life of poverty.

Three modern cases of responsive xenoglossy have been studied extensively:

"Gretchen"

Carroll Jay was a Methodist minister in Elkton, Virginia, who began using hypnosis on his wife, Dolores, in an effort to relieve her back pain. During such a session in 1970, he asked her, while she was entranced, if her back still hurt. She answered in German, *"Nein."* In a subsequent session, she began speaking German again, identifying herself as "Gretchen." Dolores Jay had never studied German.

Gretchen continued to appear in more hypnosis sessions. She understood questions put to her in very simple English, but answered only in imperfect German. She said she was Gretchen Gottlieb, daughter of the mayor of Eberswalde, Germany, who had died at about age sixteen after a severe beating. Based on her descriptions of her life, it appeared she had lived in the second half of the nineteenth century.

Dolores Jay was afraid she was being possessed by the spirit of the dead girl; she did not believe she herself had lived before as Gretchen. Some of the parapsychologists and other experts who investigated the case theorized that "Gretchen" was a fictitious personality brought forth from Jay's subconscious as a way of expressing deeply buried memories. No conclusive explanation was ever reached.

"Jensen"

Another American woman hypnotized by her husband (a physician) who began speaking an unlearned language was "T. E." (not her real initials) of Philadelphia. In sessions in 1955 and 1956, T. E. began speaking an archaic and colloquial Swedish in a deep voice. She identified herself as "Jensen," a male peasant farmer. Jensen was not fluent in his conversation; however, his diction was like that of one who speaks

171

in his native tongue. T. E. had never studied any Scandinavian language.

Jensen provided only sparse details about himself, one being that he had died after suffering a blow to the head. Interestingly, T. E. suffered from headaches. From his speech, it was deduced that Jensen had lived in the seventeenth century.

Among those who investigated the case was Ian Stevenson, who felt that T. E.'s ability to speak Swedish was indeed paranormal. Thus, the case is considered to be evidence in support of reincarnation.

"Sharada"

Uttara X., an Indian woman born in 1941, was thirty-three years old when a Bengali-speaking personality named "Sharada" manifested itself in her life. Uttara spoke Marathi, but had made an effort to learn some Bengali when she was a child; she had felt a great affinity for it. The appearance of Sharada came after a long period of physical illness and psychological stress. Over about eight years, Sharada would completely take over Uttara's life for periods lasting from a few hours to forty-one days at the longest. The spells were preceded by premonitions on the part of Uttara.

Sharada spoke fluent Bengali and sang Bengali songs. She said she was of the Brahmin caste (Uttara's family was not) and refused to believe she was dead. She had lived in the first half of the nineteenth century, was married, and had been seven months pregnant. The last thing she remembered of her life was falling unconscious after a snakebite. She woke up in the body of Uttara. She was greatly distressed to learn that her family was long dead.

Sharada favored nineteenth-century dress and mannerisms, and was much more extroverted than Uttara.

Existing records (few) indicated that a man who may have been her father died by 1827.

Prof. V. V. Akolkar, a parapsychologist of Pune, India, who investigated the case, theorizes that Uttara's regression, of which Sharada was a part, was brought on by several factors: her "extreme psychophysical exhaustion"; unfulfilled aspirations for marriage and motherhood; and the practice of meditation, which speeded her spiritual progress. Akolkar also points out that the *Bhagavad-Gita* says that persons who cannot attain the higher states of yoga are born into spiritually inclined families. The Sharada spells began to diminish when Uttara reached her forties. Akolkar said this perhaps coincided with diminished prospects for motherhood.

THE BLIND VIRTUOSO

A remarkable case of unexplained musical talent is that of "Blind Tom," a black slave of the nineteenth century. He was born blind in 1849 to a slave woman owned by Perry H. Oliver, a farmer of Muscogee County, Georgia. As a slave, the infant had no value; rather, he was a liability, a useless mouth to feed. Oliver determined to rid himself of his liability as quickly as possible, and when the boy was a year old, he put the mother on the auction block. General James Bethune of Columbus, Georgia, bought her. When the sale was completed, Oliver gleefully announced that the woman had a child who would be thrown in for free, and he produced the blind boy from a hiding spot.

Perhaps Oliver congratulated himself all the way home for his cleverness. He had no idea, however, that what he had done was a blessing for the boy. Many slave owners might have been as indifferent as Oliver, or worse, but Bethune graciously took the infant into his care. He named the child Thomas Greene Bethune.

The Bethunes were quick to observe that Blind Tom, as the boy became known, had a keen ear for music, and for all sounds in general. At age three, he astonished the household by spontaneously joining the general's daughters in song, singing perfect harmony. The Bethune girls, like all cultured young ladies at the time, studied the piano. One evening when Blind Tom was four, the girls spent several hours playing the piano in the parlor. After they departed, the boy sat down at the keyboard and played back everything he had heard. He demonstrated complete familiarity with both major and minor scales, though no one could recall him ever touching a piano. His fingers rippled up and down the keyboard with the confidence of a seasoned artist.

General Bethune attempted to get formal instruction for Blind Tom, but Carlo Patti, one of the leading musicians in Columbus and the Bethune girls' teacher, declined, saying the boy knew more about music than he. "All that can be done for him will be to let him hear fine playing; he will work it out by himself," Patti said.

Blind Tom began giving public concerts at age eight. During the Civil War, he entertained troops on both sides with the music of the great classical composers. He gave concerts in Britain, Europe, and in the White House. In addition to his talent for playing by ear, Blind Tom demonstrated considerable prowess in improvisation. Critics and reviewers were amazed at his mastery of music, a mastery that seemed to come from the very essence of his soul.

No explanation ever satisfactorily explained how a blind, uneducated slave boy could possess such brilliant musical gifts. Perhaps reincarnation is the only plausible theory.

Stevenson has found indications of skill carryover in many of the childhood cases of spontaneous reincarnation memories that he has investigated. Such children display at a very early age interests or skills that they could not readily have learned from older persons, either through instruction or imitation. The children say that they remember using the skills in a previous life. Corliss Chotkin, Jr., mentioned in Chapter Seven, claimed to be his deceased uncle born again, and as a child, displayed remarkable skill in handling and repairing marine engines without having been taught. Corliss's father had no such interest or skill, but his deceased uncle had been very fond of boats and engines.

It is possible that children tap into past-life memories without being aware of it when they play at some imaginary occupation. The child who sets up a restaurant or pretends to be a horse trainer with persistent and amazing passion is perhaps acting out a drama from the past. Consider the following story:

FOREVER A FIGHTER

George Smith Patton, Jr., the tough American general whose brilliant command of the Third Army in World War II helped liberate France in 1944 and defeat Germany in 1945, knew from childhood that he would be a soldier. He was certain of that not only because the Patton lineage included many illustrious military men, but because he possessed a mysterious sense of having lived as a soldier many times before. As he grew older, he came to believe that his military skills had been honed over a series of lifetimes dating back to classical times.

Patton believed in a God of Battles, and felt it was his destiny to be a soldier in lifetime after lifetime, cheered on by a spirit host of ancestors. He once told his nephew, Fred Ayer, Jr., who wrote a biography of his uncle titled *Before the Colors Fade*, that there was no question that he believed in reincarnation. "I don't just think it, I damn well know there are places I've been before, and not in this life," Patton said.

To illustrate, Patton told of his first command in France in Langres, a town with Roman roots, which Patton had never before visited. A French liaison officer offered to show him around, but Patton stunned the young man by telling him he knew the place well. As the two drove around, Patton gave directions, feeling as though someone were whispering them in his ear. He knew the way to the sites of the town's Roman amphitheater, forum, and temples of Mars and Apollo, even though some of the structures no longer existed. He also found the military drill ground and the spot where Caesar had once pitched his tent. He knew the town so well, he said, because he had been there himself as a soldier in Caesar's Tenth Legion, and he could still smell the sweat of the men and feel himself mingling with the Roman crowds.

Patton often surprised others with his past-life beliefs. Once in Africa during World War II, Sir Harold Alexander of England remarked to him, "You know, George, you would have made a great marshal for Napoleon if you'd lived in the eighteenth century." "I did," Patton replied.

Patton believed he had fought with the Greeks against the Trojans in the Trojan War, had served under Alexander the Great at Tyre, had fought against the Huns as they invaded Europe, had fought with the Crusaders in the Holy Land, had served Henry V at Agincourt, and had served with the Scottish Highlanders of the House of Stuart. He had battled on the side of Napoleon at Jena and fought for the Confederates in the American Civil War at Winchester and Gettysburg. Patton's sense of having fought in battles throughout the centuries gave him an exceptional gift for planning strategies. He felt that the spirits of all these warriors were impressed into his blood and soul, preparing him in his most recent life for one of his greatest and most important roles, helping to ensure the defeat of Hitler's Nazi machine.

Patton succinctly summarized his views about his many lives and his destiny in his poem "Through A Glass Darkly," which he wrote in 1944, a year before he died. He wrote that he had fought in many guises and under many names, but always for God's will. His destiny was to be forever reborn a fighter.

Many modern reincarnationists believe that times of great crisis are foreseen and planned for on the other side of the veil, and that reincarnations are prepared so that the appropriately developed souls descend into the flesh in order to provide the needed leadership.

Edgar Cayce said that each entity must have spiritual ideals, or purposes, for entering into each life experience. The ideals help the soul, through their mental and material associations and activities, to grow in grace, knowledge, and understanding. The abilities of the soul that are manifested on earth must be used in service to others for the glorification of the Creative Force and not for self. The channels of expression in a given life depend in part upon the channels used by the soul in previous lives. Patton's example certainly supports Cayce's views.

The Cayce readings contain many examples of skills and talents built up over lifetimes. That is not to say that every soul returns to the same task in life after life; the primary occupation may be separated by lives in unrelated jobs, in order, for example, to balance the soul's karma. In many cases, a soul develops skills by serving in a variety of related occupations. For example, one Cayce client was a successful osteopathic physician whose skills could be attributed to at least three past lives: one as a doctor who worked closely with Native Americans and learned their natural and herbal lore; one as a supervisor of baths and massages in early Christian times; and one in ancient Egypt as an embalmer. Similarly, a New York composer and arranger had past lives as a music teacher, a carver of wooden musical instruments, a buffoon in the court of King Nebuchadnezzar, and an Atlantean who worked in sacred music.

In her book *Many Mansions,* Gina Cerminara observed that vocations are both "the matrix through which some aspect of man's spiritual growth takes place" and a crucial part of the realm of matter that must be mastered by the spirit. Perhaps the mastery of vocation is necessary for man to become a co-creator with God, "a poised, pure, and potent spirit, a harmless, radiant, loving, and creative center of expression, capable himself of generating forms and lives and worlds."

The question naturally arises as to when and how a soul decides to pursue certain vocations. Unfortunately, Cayce provided no definite answers, although his readings show that souls do change their vocations and interests. In analyzing Cayce's readings, Cerminara found that changes seem to come about through two forces of equal strength—desire and karmic law. A person may have experiences in one lifetime that inspire new directions, or a change may be necessary to balance the soul's karma. It may take several lifetimes to make the transition to a new vocation. This may perhaps explain why some people are more successful in their fields than others, though the idea should never be used as an excuse for lack of initiative or poor performance. Whatever conditions and obstacles are present in a given life, the soul always must strive to fulfill its destiny and attain its highest potential.

People who experience difficulties or failures in their vocations sometimes find the causes in past lives. Invariably, the present problems are karmic repayment for past abuses of a spiritual nature. Cerminara tells of one Cayce client, a man suffering from an increasing distaste for the social requirements of his job as a real estate agent. Cayce told him that in a past life he had been a rigid, harsh, and dictatorial teacher, and now was learning a lesson in relating to others. Cayce advised him to stay in his vocation and absorb the lesson.

Professional problems are one of the main reasons people seek out past-life counseling, according to Alice T., the Manhattan regressionist: "They feel very talented, capable, and qualified for the work they're doing, yet they're having little success. Everything is a struggle; nothing is easy. The cause often turns out to be a past life in which they were successful and powerful and abused their position in some way. Sometimes it's guilt—they think they abused their power or failed others by not helping them and, therefore, they do not deserve to be successful in this life." Discovering the roots of problems like these in past lives can help a person to cope or to find a solution.

THE FABERGÉ JEWELER

Past-life vocations that are not vocations in the present life often reappear as hobbies, strong interests, and leisure pursuits. Michael Talbot, the Manhattan writer who developed the Resonance Method of past-life recall (see Chapter Two), had always had a resonance for Russia, but hadn't pinned it down to a time period. He pieced together fragments, "almost like a detective story," as he described the process. One key piece fell into place one day while he was out walking on Central Park West, and had a spontaneous memory concerning St. Petersburg during the time of czarist Russia. The memory was touched off by his recollection of a Smirnoff vodka ad he'd seen in a magazine, which showed a gilt-framed portrait of one of the czars. Talbot recounted:

What hit me was that the picture frame had cost a lot of money, and who had stolen it [from me]? I was instantly outraged. I was on my way back to my apartment to search for it when I thought, "What on earth am I thinking?" I have not owned a beautifully framed portrait of the czar in this lifetime. I then experienced visual images of a large and beautiful house in St. Petersburg. I knew that in this past life, I was a man. I carried a cane. I can almost feel it in my hands. I didn't need it for walking—it was more for style. I had a strong sense of riding around in carriages, and that my father in this life was there.

I knew that I had been a jeweler before, but I hadn't pieced it together with the Russian life. I have a fascination for building miniatures, and I've always tinkered with watches and other small objects. When friends' eyeglasses and things like that break, they bring them to me for repairs. When I was fourteen, I was in a bookstore and saw a book on Fabergé [Peter Carl Fabergé, 1846–1920, the Russian goldsmith famed for the elegant jewelry and exotic Easter eggs he designed for the royal family]. I was riveted to it, but nothing bubbled up enough in my subconscious for me to question why I was so interested—at that age I wasn't looking for past-life information. Yet I knew that name.

Psychic Jim Gordon gave Talbot additional information, telling him that he had lived in St. Petersburg just before the Russian Revolution of 1917, and was trained as a jeweler in the house of Fabergé. However, he'd never worked as a jeweler, because his family had money. His present father had been his uncle in that life, and the uncle's two sons, both of whom had fought in the war, were now Talbot's nephews in the present. Without knowing about his son's past-life recollections, Talbot's father revealed that he had a feeling he had once lived in Russia.

> My father had a dream that he was shot during the Russian Revolution. He didn't know which side he was on, but someone was after him and was going to shoot him. He ran in front of this beautiful marble building, and he thought they wouldn't shoot him there because they wouldn't want to injure the building. They shot him anyway. Later, he was watching a television special on Russia and saw the same beautiful marble building. There were bullet holes in the building because during the revolution, people had been shot in front of it.

If yesterday's occupations form today's hobbies, then it is just as likely that today's hobby may become one's vocation in future lives.

CHAPTER TWELVE

The Traveling Interplanetary Musician

While some people turn to their past lives in hopes of solving career problems, many more do so to find new careers altogether. "An amazing number of people seek past-life therapy because they want to make a career change but don't know what they should do," said regressionist Alice T. "They aren't sure where their talents lie. What we do is look at a past life that reveals the person's strengths in practical areas. If you live in a city, it's not going to be useful to find out you once were a terrific blacksmith. When we investigate careers in past lives, we are somehow able to call upon latent talent more clearly. Talent is yours forever. It's just a matter of finding a way to awaken it." One career seeker who came to see Alice was Ornyece Prince.

Prince has a composure and style that most people would envy. A striking woman, she can carry off wearing distinctive clothing and jewelry with grace. It comes as no surprise, then, to learn that Prince has worked in fashion virtually all her professional life, as a designer of costumes for the theater. In 1986, she launched her own line of jewelry, a business she manages from her home in New York City.

To the casual observer, it might seem that Prince had carved out a nice niche of independence. Deep down inside, however, she felt something was not right about her life, that she was not in the right place doing the right thing. Meeting with me over coffee in Manhattan, she confided that she has felt this way for a long time, and it has left her quite frustrated. Despite her work as an artist, she'd always had the odd feeling of being in service to others. "While it's good to serve people," she acknowledged, "I have always felt that I was here to pay some sort of a humbling debt. I've wanted to find out why."

Prince had glimpsed previous lives and had encountered dark mysteries at an early age. She came into the world feet first, her large, thirteen-pound, eleven-ounce body covered from head to toe with weeping eczema from a dry birth. The eczema gave her skin the appearance of having been burned. From the earliest moment she can remember, she was aware of the presence of a spirit woman.

I used to see this woman all the time. She had a German shepherd. She was very pale and had dark hair, and she was very still and peaceful. Her hair was cut in a pageboy and she wore a shirtwaist dress. She would just stand there with the dog. Sometimes I would walk around a corner and see her. She wouldn't be looking at me, but I knew she was there for me, there was a connection. I never tried to think it out, I tried to think it away. I was never afraid of her, I thought it was normal. She never spoke to me or did anything. If

I mentioned her to my family, it caused such an uproar that I thought there was something wrong, something bad about it.

By the time Prince reached her teens, the woman had ceased to appear, but the German shepherd remained. "Even after I was a grown woman and had my son, I would walk down a corridor and swear I saw a dog, and then suddenly it wasn't there anymore," she remembers.

Years later, Prince thought the spirit woman might have been an aspect of herself, or a former self from another life. Her son told her once he was afraid that one day he would walk into a room and see that she had been replaced by a woman who resembled the Walt Disney character Cruella, a pale woman with dark hair and long nails. The Cruella woman would then try to convince him that she was now his mother. "When my son told me about this woman, I asked him to describe her. He said she had entered his dreams occasionally when he was very young. It's the same woman I used to see when I was a child," Prince said. She has encountered the woman again in her past-life regressions.

Also during childhood, Prince spoke of believing in reincarnation and the possibility of intelligent life on other planets, which left her father, a conservative minister, aghast. "To shut me up, he would say, 'That can't be God speaking, it must be the Devil,' " Prince said. Like many children who learn it's not appropriate to speak of past lives, Prince began to keep quiet about her private thoughts.

For most of her life, Prince had lived with a vivid memory of once being a wise woman who lived in a forest with a little boy. Both of them were burned alive because others believed she was a witch. The little boy was her father in the present life. Here is her story:

I stayed away from people—they came to me. They knew about me through word of mouth. I was a healer. I lived in a covered wagon with a lot of shelves and pouches and glass jars with herbs and things. I had clairvoyance, but it seemed natural. I was a peaceful, young person, I would say between the ages of seventeen and twenty-eight. One day this little boy found me where I lived at a campsite. I don't know if he ran away or was lost, but he tried to give me the impression that he was just a loner. He didn't want to be returned to wherever he came from. I wound up being a mentor to him. I would tell him about spiritual things, and how things could not happen to you unless you allow them to happen.

Somehow the wrong people found out I was living there, and they looked on me as a witch. They were going to burn me at the stake. I was tied to a stake or a tree, with dried grass or bushes around me, and the boy was tied to my left. He was looking at me, starting to panic and cry. I tried to tell him telepathically that everything was all right, that he was going to be okay and not to worry. He looked at me and trusted me. We both still burned. In his passing on, I think he was confused, that he was registering my teaching about spirituality on a mundane level. He really thought that something was going to happen to rescue him and he would not burn, and that was not what I was trying to get across.

In this life, my father and I battled from day one. I could never understand how a man could look at a little child and say such negative things. In this life, he was not going to listen to me. He, a minister, was sure of everything he said. In effect, he was telling me, "Now it's *your* turn to listen to *me*."

Prince also recognized a connection between her death by burning in that life and her arrival in this life looking as though she had been burned.

Questions about her relationships and her true purpose in life led Prince to Alice. Prince didn't know what to expect from viewing past lives. She asked to see a life in which she possessed a skill or talent that enabled her to lead a completely satisfying life—professionally, spiritually, financially, and emotionally. It was her hope that she would unlock creative energies deep within herself that would help her redirect her present professional activities. She also had another question: Why was she such a procrastinator? The life that was revealed in answer caught her so completely by surprise that she at first did not know how to respond.

Alice, using guided meditation, relaxed Prince and directed her to drift back in time through a dark tunnel. When she stepped out of the tunnel, Prince was astonished to find herself on what seemed to be another planet. And she was not human, but an odd, large, humanoid being. "I feel I'm a creature!" she said, bemused, when Alice asked if she was male or female. "I think it may be male."

She took in the scene before her bit by bit. She saw it from both the viewpoint of herself and the viewpoint of this creature. The creature—Prince dubbed him "Og"—had his huge, wide feet planted on a flat, vast plain that shimmered in metallic hues of blue, gray, and silver. The sky was colored the same metallic hues, and so were objects that might have been clouds. She thought there was no sun, moon, trees, or large rocks. The only land formations were small mounds that rose up from the plain, which seemed to stretch on forever.

It dawned on Prince that the metallic hues represented Og's vision, like a person who is color-blind seeing only certain colors. Looking down at Og's feet, she saw he wore brown sandals, yet Og saw them in the same metallic colors that bathed everything else, including his skin. His clothing consisted of a tattered toga, which registered also as a metallic, silvery blue.

His humanoid feet were wide, about nine inches across. Prince gazed in fascination at his toes. Og seemed fascinated, too, and very proud of an ornament that appeared to be a gold nugget on the nail of one outer toe. It seemed to be a symbol of achievement.

Og's entire body was thick and wide, like his feet. He was at least nine feet tall. His face was large with bold features. His hair was coarse and silvery gray, almost like steel wool in consistency, and piled high on his head.

Prince sense a great deal of gentleness and pride within Og, despite his imposing physique. He felt secure, yet he was of limited intellect—so limited that Prince felt embarrassed for him. He seemed to be very old, even thousands of years old, yet was young at the same time, as though many, many Earth years represented a short time to beings of his race.

As Og stared out over the shimmering plain, Prince realized that he had 360-degree vision and that she could see everything behind as well as in front of her. What was he doing in this place? she wondered. With one hand, he was leaning upon a cylindrical object. His other hand held a strange tool or instrument. It was taller than he and was unlike anything Prince had ever seen. It was shaped like a half-U. The straight portion had separations or perhaps strings and was pierced by pegs or frets. The bottom, curved portion seemed to be computerized, with buttons and bars.

Prince tried to get Og to move, but he wouldn't budge. Gold stairs appeared in front of him, leading up to a building with pillars. Og registered the golden color as the same narrow band of metallic hues. Prince knew there were other beings in the building, though she neither saw nor heard them. When Og still refused to move, Prince and her regressionist decided to leave that life and go on to another.

Afterward, Prince felt a bit disappointed that the regression hadn't given her the answers she had sought to her professional situation. Og was intriguing, but what did it all mean? He had simply stood there, grasping his weird object, refusing to budge.

Sometimes the energies and information unlocked by a past-life regression do not appear immediately, but bubble up slowly to the conscious mind. Prince went home, listened to the tape recording of her regression session, and put it out of her thoughts.

Some time later, she attended an opening night party for a film. There she met a famous singer who was making his acting debut in the film. Impulsively, she asked him if he would be interested in setting to music some poems she had written. He agreed to take a look at them.

Back home, Prince examined her poems and found them too personal. She decided to try her hand at writing some fresh lyrics. The words came effortlessly and, to her surprise, so did the melodies, though she had never written a song before. Though most of her immediate family had studied classical music and one of her aunts was an opera singer, Prince had never had the slightest interest in learning about music. She had never taken a single lesson, and knew nothing about composing.

But now the melodies were pouring into her head, compelling her to set them down. She fetched her son's electronic keyboard, took a soft pencil, and wrote the scale letters on the keys. As she composed the music, she jotted down the letters on a piece of paper. In this crude fashion, she quickly finished three songs.

The singer declined further involvement, but for Prince, it was only the beginning. Songwriting was fast becoming an obsession. She made inquiries through friends and contacts and found a musician who agreed to teach her how to compose music formally. She told him she knew nothing, but he hardly believed her. Not only did she have perfect pitch, he said, but she knew enough to appear trained in music. Prince shrugged it off. "Maybe it's because I grew up in a musical home," she said. "I just never thought I was paying attention."

One night, Prince played her regression tape again and fell asleep while listening to it. Through her dreams, the pieces of the puzzle of Og began falling into place.

I began to understand him and recognize things. Og was an interplanetary, traveling musician, and this thing he held in his hand was his instrument. The cylindrical object next to him was his ship. When he traveled to different places and landed, he didn't move until he was sure it was okay, especially if the place was new to him. That answered my question about why I procrastinate.

This particular place in my regression was known for war, so he didn't feel that secure. It was the demilitarized zone where nothing would happen, but he had to be sure. He had to know who was sending for him, and if their intentions were honorable. The instrument was complex, but not to him. It had special tones that most people couldn't handle, but they loved the music and felt it was worth sending for someone like Og to entertain them. He was known as the best.

I put two and two together that perhaps I am

supposed to be in the music field, and that my success will eventually come in music. I went to a producer with a demo tape. I didn't tell him it was mine, but said it belonged to a friend of mine who was a musician. He listened to the tape and was impressed. The first thing he said was, "This is different, very different. As a matter of fact, I don't know where to place this music. Maybe it's the kind of music that has to go to Europe first and then come back here because people won't be ready to understand it, it's too different. Yet it has a good beat and it's danceable."

The producer told Prince he wanted to hear more samples, and she set out to work. At the close of 1988, she had copyrighted nine songs, and was exhilarated with the new creative energy she had found. Though she was still earning her living from her jewelry, she foresaw a time when she would live from the proceeds of her music.

Prince's exploration of past-life regression answered one other key question: Why did she feel part of her purpose in this life was to repay a debt of humbleness? The answer came in the form of a woman Prince had been over and over again: tall, slender, regal in bearing, cool, aloof, distant—and very much alone.

Prince regressed to a life in which she was a wealthy, assertive businesswoman. She owned a shop that sold imported and handmade fashionable clothing, and she traveled extensively in her business dealings. She lived with a bevy of servants in a luxurious mansion, where she hosted elegant balls. In her pillared ballroom of ivory and gold, she danced in her pink satin and tulle dress and white satin pumps. It was a busy life, well planned and controlled, her calendar jammed with commitments—but she had no emotional ties.

The woman surfaced in another life, in a primitive setting that appeared to be in the Middle East. She was tall and thin with caramel-colored skin, and acted as ruler and judge over her people. She lived in an ivory and gold palace with marble stairs; one upper window looked out over the marketplace of the city. Accused criminals and violators of the law were brought to her for sentencing. She was in her thirties and wise beyond her years.

As this life unfolded, a man was kneeling before her, trying to explain his transgression and begging for mercy in a pitiful voice. The scene shifted, and Prince saw another man brought before her. He had been on a rampage through the marketplace, knocking over carts and damaging merchandise. Prince recognized him in that life as a known thief, con man, and liar. She also recognized him from the present life: he was yet again a con man, and had tried to convince her to enter into a business deal with him.

As the judge, Prince sentenced the man to have his head cut off. The punishment was not solely for his destruction in the marketplace. Prince was made aware that the man had intended to cause her harm, and that he had planned the marketplace incident as a way to gain access to the palace. She never watched executions, but for some reason, she decided to witness this one, which was carried out immediately.

After the execution, she went upstairs to an ornate room with a cot or bed, window seats, and a table with a bowl of fruit on it. She lay down on the cot and contemplated suicide. Her life as a judge of others overwhelmed her and seemed pointless. She had no regrets about the punishments she'd meted out, but she no longer desired to be a judge. She felt cold-hearted and depressed. She got up and went to the table. The bowl contained red berries, which were poisonous and which she kept on hand in anticipation of just such a moment. She had thought about suicide for a long time. She took the berries and sat on the window seat, where she could watch the bustle of the city as she ate the poisonous fruit. People walked about with huge loaves of bread on their shoulders and pushed carts laden with fruit and hay. The noise wafted up to her window. She felt dreamy. She knew it was wrong to take her own life, but she was bored and tired of it, tired of answering the demands of her people, who, she felt, forced her to punish them for their wrongdoing and never seemed to learn anything from it. She was so self-assured that she felt she could control what happened to her as she passed on—that she would not go to hell, but would go to the light. She would shed this life and move into another existence. As the poison began to take effect, Prince was shocked to find she had no control over her transition.

Everything became dark and got as dark as navy blue. I never saw a light. That did throw me. I felt I could still change things and go to the light, but it wasn't happening. I remained in this state in the dark. It was pulsating like electricity. It was a void. I was thrown because for the first time I was not in a position to control things, [make them be] the way I wanted them to be. I stayed in this limbo for an indefinite time and then was released into another life.

There always was a person inside of me who felt she was in control and had this power that put her above the spiritual laws. I have never had a relationship that was fulfilling. I found out through this woman that just being judgmental can distance me from others. I've always felt I'm not judgmental, but I guess I am, to a certain extent.

I noticed that in every life, I didn't see a lot of people around me. I was alone. I had position, I didn't love intimately, and I didn't have domestic responsibilities—I always had someone to do that for me. There were a lot of people around who were servants, rather than friends or relatives. Even Og was a loner. It seemed as if he didn't need much in life. He didn't have an entourage— he traveled alone. His space capsule seemed to seat one or two persons.

In analyzing what she had learned from her past lives, Prince still felt a need to be in control but realized that that in itself would not necessarily bring her everything she wanted. She appreciated the strength and assertiveness of the "power woman," but not her judging of others. She felt she could integrate the best characteristics of that woman and Og into her present life. "I haven't the right to judge anyone," she concluded. "It only causes disharmony with others as well as with oneself. From Og, I have learned that livelihood and contentment should be synonymous."

CHAPTER THIRTEEN

The Past-Life Muse

Those who work in the creative arts have various theories as to the source of their inspiration and ideas. A majority believe they are somehow influenced by supernormal forces. Some believe their inspiration is divine, while others believe they are aided by spirit guides or spirits of the dead. Some feel their inspiration comes from their own imagination triggered or enhanced by guiding forces. Some believe they tap into some sort of cosmic current, while still others believe that they tap into their own past lives. Perhaps all of those possibilities, and more, come into play.

In his book *An Encyclopedia of Psychic Science*, the respected psychoanalyst and psychical researcher Nandor Fodor defines inspiration as "a psychic state in which one becomes susceptible to creative spiritual influence, or, to a varying degree, unwittingly lends oneself as an instrument for thought-flowing ideas." Mozart and Beethoven were among those stellar composers who felt blessed by a mysterious inspiration. Mozart described how thoughts streamed in on him at certain times, when he was in a relaxed state or when he could not sleep at night. Beethoven felt that his inspiration came from an exalted state of awareness in which he felt the intertwined harmony of all things.

Henry David Thoreau, the Transcendentalist whose famous works include *Walden* and the essay "Civil Disobedience," studied Hindu philosophy and the concepts of karma and reincarnation, which were reflected in his philosophical writings. He wrote in *Walden and Miscellaneous Writings* that the hawk had earned his power of flight "by faithfully creeping on the ground in a former state of existence." Of his own past lives, Thoreau stated in a letter to Harrison Blake that the sky at night in New England looked the same to him as it had when he was a shepherd in Assyria. In other letters to Blake and to Ralph Waldo Emerson, published in Thoreau's *Letters and Journals,* he said:

> I lived in Judea eighteen hundred years ago, but I never knew there was such a one as Christ among my contemporaries. . . .
> And [Nathaniel] Hawthorne too, I remember as one with whom I sauntered in old heroic times among the banks of the Scamander amid the ruins of chariots and heroes. . . . As far back as I can remember I have unconsciously referred to the experiences of a previous state of existence.

Louisa May Alcott also believed she had lived before. In a letter she wrote:

> I think immortality is the passing of a soul through many lives or experiences; and such as are truly lived, used, and learned, help on to the next, each growing richer, happier, and higher, carrying with it only the real memories of what

has gone before. . . . I seem to remember former states and feel that in them I have learned some of the lessons that have never since been mine here and in my next step I hope to leave behind many of the trials I have struggled to bear here and begin to find lightened as I go on. This accounts for the genius and great virtue some show here.

Inspiration is of particular interest to writers, especially novelists, who create characters and worlds and make them real. Whence do these fantasy people and their worlds come? William Makepeace Thackeray once admitted surprise at some of the things his characters had to say. "It seems as if an occult power was moving the pen," he wrote in 1862. "The personage does or says something and I ask: 'How did he come to think of that?' " Though Thackeray himself did not speculate upon past lives, perhaps novelists are attuned more than others to past lives, consciously or unconsciously, because they create imaginary worlds.

JOAN GRANT'S PAST-LIFE BIOGRAPHIES

London-born Joan Grant did not turn to writing until she discovered her past lives. In 1937, at age thirty, she published the first of seven novels that she said were essentially the biographies of her own past lives. The wealth of information she presented in these novels, she said, was obtained in an enhanced recall technique she called "far memory," which she described as the displacement of a major portion of her consciousness from her present life to a past life. In this altered state, she became her past self, and dictated what was happening to her as she relived bits and pieces of that previous life. Her far memory sessions sometimes lasted for hours. She never knew what she was going to see, and had to fit her pieces together later in order to relate a chronological tale.

Grant's incredible ability to tune in to her past was a product of her innate psychic gifts. As a small child, she was aware of having other selves; she possessed some memory of four male and three female previous lives, including that of a young Greek boy who was a runner. By the age of eleven, she was having strange dreams, some precognitive and others in which she was another, much older person who helped the newly dead cross over to the other side. During World War I, she dreamed of being a nurse on a battlefield, telling soldiers they were dead and helping them on their way. In her waking hours, she could perceive ghosts, and received piano lessons from a dead woman's spirit. Her contact with the spirit world increased through use of the planchette, a device with a pencil used to produce automatic writing.

After her marriage to Leslie Grant, a barrister, in 1927, she vowed to get a better understanding of her connection to the unseen, and began recording her dreams. She learned psychometry, a psychic skill in which visions and other sensory information is derived by handling an object (a psychometrized ring, for example, may yield information about its owner).

In 1935, the Grants went on an archaeological dig in Iran, where Grant put her psychometry skill to use in handling Sumerian artifacts. She would touch an object to the middle of her forehead, the site of the third eye, and immediately see moving images from the past. In 1936, when a close friend named Daisy gave her some Egyptian scarabs to psychometrize, Grant discovered Sekeeta, daughter of a pharaoh.

At first, Grant did not realize she had tuned in to one of her own past lives. Her sense of identification with Sekeeta intensified, until she realized that this was the explanation. Daisy had been Sekeeta's mother. Initially, Grant continued to use the scarab as the stimulus for reaching Sekeeta. Eventually she was able to teach herself the far memory technique, in which her "I" expanded and became the subject of the past life. She learned how to distinguish imagination from recall: the details of a recall, she said, could not be changed, no matter how hard she tried.

In the story that unfolded, Grant learned that Sekeeta had spent ten years in a temple, training to be a Winged Pharaoh, a ruler and healer. Sekeeta herself had learned far memory as one of the skills necessary for leadership. She was required to remember at least ten of her own deaths, so that she would be able to comfort the dying. Her initiation test for far memory was to spend four days and nights in a tomblike chamber, during which she left her body to see other levels of reality. Sekeeta also had to undergo seven initiatory ordeals to test her courage. In the Seventh Ordeal, she had to fight a huge cobra. It was a terrifying experience, all the more traumatic for Grant because of her own fear of snakes. The recall left her so physically shaken and exhaused that she suffered headaches, cramps, and fever for two days.

Grant collected 200 episodes from the life of Sekeeta and wove them into her first novel, *Winged Pharaoh,* published in 1937. Sekeeta's world sprang to life in minute and colorful detail. Interestingly, Grant had visited Egypt prior to discovering Sekeeta, and had felt no déjà vu. As her past-life explorations continued over the years, she recalled numerous lives in ancient Egypt.

Material for her second novel, *Life as Carola,* spilled out unexpectedly when a friend asked Grant if she could simultaneously hear Egyptian music while listening to harpsichord music by Haydn. Grant "shifted level," as she called her entrance into far memory. When she returned to full consciousness, she was told she had given details of a past life as Carola di Ludovici, a sixteenth-century Italian girl who played the lute and died at the age of twenty-seven. The harpsichord music apparently had triggered the connection.

Grant's newfound literary success contributed to the breakup of her marriage, for her husband was ill at ease with the subjects of her study. It was one thing to entertain friends in the parlor with psychometry, quite another to go public with a book. Leslie Grant was a man concerned with appearances, and with what the members of his club would say.

Grant returned to Egypt for the subject of her next two far memory novels, *Eyes of Horus* and *Lords of the Horizon*. She had lived 1,000 years after Sekeeta in the last reign of the Eleventh Dynasty as Ra-ab Hotep, the Nomarch (the equivalent of a lord lieutenant in England) of the Oryx. Ra-ab Hotep belonged to the Eyes of Horus, a resistance movement fighting against the corrupt priesthood. According to Grant, his family's tombs do exist and are located at Beni Hasan in Egypt.

Scarlet Feather, Grant's fifth far-memory novel, recounts a female life in North America in the second millennium before Christ, in which she underwent the ordeals of male warriors and earned the right to wear the sacred scarlet feather. *Return to Elysium* tells the story of Lucina, a Greek girl of the second century B.C. who was the ward of a philosopher who preached against immortality. Lucina, who, like Grant's other incarnations, retained far memory, knew this was not true. After convincing the philosopher that he was wrong, she left him to establish her own practice on an island in the Tiber.

Grant's last novel, *So Moses Was Born*, is set in Egypt and concerns a male contemporary of Rameses

II. Published in 1958, it was her last past-life biography. All seven novels remain popular to this day.

In 1958, Grant shifted away from her novels and into psychotherapy. She met Denys Kelsey, a psychiatrist and hypnotherapist, who became her second husband. The two established a practice in which Grant used her far memory to validate the past-life recalls of patients under hypnosis. Regression was employed when Kelsey believed the cause of a neurosis, phobia, or guilt feeling might lie in the past. Grant's ability to tune in to the patients' recalls enabled her to sort out true recall from fantasies, the latter of which she said appeared to her as static, while recalls were active.

According to Grant, man has four phases of evolution, spending many lifetimes in each phase as his consciousness expands. Beginning as a molecule of energy, he graduates to the mineral kingdom, then to the plant kingdom, then to the animal kingdom, and finally to the human realm. As a human, his consciousness eventually expands so that it becomes too large for a single personality, and an incarnation includes both a personality and a component of his total self.

MICHAEL TALBOT'S PAST-LIFE INSPIRATION

Manhattan author Michael Talbot, who writes both nonfiction and fiction, feels that pieces of his own past lives become material for his novels.

> Frequently when I write, past-life material channels through, I think. I don't go into a trance, but somehow I tap into the past. I think this is true of writers in general. We draw upon what we know although we think it's imagination.
>
> I wrote a book called *The Delicate Dependency,* a vampire horror novel that takes place in

the 1890s. I wrote a lot of stuff I thought was purely out of my imagination. It turned out to be taken from past-life memories.

One character is a monk who is a wandering troubadour. I discovered later that this came from a past life I had in the 1500s in which I was a troubadour, a mountebank like Cagliostro, who knew mystical things. I courted a beautiful woman, whom I also know in this life. She saw through me, that I was a bit of a charlatan. Through gossip she destroyed me, and I was imprisoned and died of a lung infection. All of those things have resonance for me: being a troubadour, being in prison, dying of a lung infection.

In the novel, I made the troubadour monk a vampire. The reason I wanted to write a vampire novel was that I wanted to write about immortality and how being immortal would change your consciousness. When I assess anything in this life, I find I'm always looking at other lives. I think it gives me a really odd take on life in general. I don't feel either young or old, but in a way I've always felt really old. My family has always commented on it. My parents have always said I was never a little boy, I was always a little man. So I thought that if you really had lived for centuries, it would change you; a 900-year-old is not the same intellectually or emotionally as a 30-year-old person.

[In the book] the vampires are very respectful of life. They have a coterie of humans that they feed on, but they loathe killing because a brutal and violent act is the only thing that can bring an end to their own lives. The thing they're most intrigued by is knowledge. Because they live for so long, they have the opportunity to study things in a way few humans can.

I seem to have drawn on my past life as the troubadour to make the monk vampire like the Illuminati or an alchemist. In one place, he says there is a secret language written into the doors of Notre Dame [cathedral]. I thought I was making it up. Later I read that it was believed that alchemists had put a secret language on the original doors of Notre Dame. These vampires met under the rose window of Notre Dame. I thought I was making that up, too. One day I was looking through the dictionary and saw the term *sub rosa*. In Latin it literally means "under the rose," and refers to a meeting held in secret.

The main character [of the book] is a British virologist who forms a hypothesis after he encounters a vampire that vampires may be victims of some sort of virus. In the course of his searching, he is incarnated in a house on the Île Saint-Louis by this 900-year-old vampire. The vampire says that he can't let the virologist go now that he has broken into the vampire's home, because the vampire's life depends on people not knowing about him. He guards the virologist with a trained falcon. The doctor knows that if he gets ripped by the bird's talons he will die. Later, in going through some of my old stories and poems, I found I had written about a trained falcon many times before and I hadn't even realized it. My hypothesis is that in some past life this had a meaning. One past life that has left a powerful resonance with me is a life in ancient Persia, where falconry was important.

Taylor Caldwell's Past Lives

Janet Taylor Caldwell, who wrote as Taylor Caldwell, penned a number of best-selling historical novels that brimmed with information she did not consciously possess. At age six, she exhibited her first inkling of reincarnation when she was handed *The Mill on the Floss,* one of the novels of the Victorian writer George Eliot (pseudonym of Mary Ann Evans). She had never read the book, yet without opening it discussed the plot in detail and said the book was "my favorite book over all the others I have written."

A prolific and imaginative writer from an early age, Caldwell at twelve began work on a novel (later published as *Dear and Glorious Physician*) of the life of St. Luke, who healed in the tradition of Hippocrates. Throughout childhood and into her adult years, she was plagued by an intense, recurring nightmare of being imprisoned by Dominican monks in a Mediterranean city. In this dream, just before three men entered her cell to torture her, she flung herself out the window and rolled down a steep, tiled roof. At this point, she invariably woke up screaming and crying.

Caldwell met with literary success in adulthood. Unusually, book after book was filled with explicit details of life in earlier times, and the personalities and actions of great people, including Christ and those around him. Her knowledge of medicine and healing in particular astounded doctors. Caldwell sensed an unseen presence that gave her inspiration, and she also believed she might have tapped into genetic memory. She very deliberately rejected the idea of reincarnation, calling it a "curse" of whatever gods might exist. She said the "very thought of it horrifies me."

Nevertheless, she was persuaded by writer Jess Stearn to undergo hypnotic regression after the death of her beloved husband, Marcus Reback, in 1970. In a series of deep-trance sessions, Caldwell journeyed back, reliving previous incarnations. She assumed the personalities, mannerisms, speech, and voices of her previous selves. Stearn's account, *The Search for a Soul: Taylor Caldwell's Psychic Lives*, was published in 1972.

Caldwell's knowledge of Christ apparently derived from a life she described as Hannah bat Joseph, mother of Mary Magdalen. She called Jesus "Yeshua ben Joseph," and recounted how he rescued her daughter from stoning by the Pharisees, who called the girl a harlot. Hannah died before Christ was crucified, but at the moment of her death, her heart burst into fire and she had a wonderful vision of him as the Messiah. He was clothed in lightning, larger than life, with rays of light streaming from his hands. His eyes were more brilliant than the brightest star, and his hair and beard were like golden fire.

Her ancient medical expertise was learned in Greece, where she'd lived as Helena, an attendant of Aphrodite, goddess of love. Helena was a kind of courtesan who worked in the house of Aspasia, the mistress of Pericles, in the fifth century B.C. As leader of Athens, Pericles brought Greek civilization to its zenith. Many learned and famous men visited Aspasia, including a physician, Heracleus, who took an interest in fifteen-year-old Helena after he set her broken arm. He taught her the healing arts and sent her to school disguised as a man, for women were not allowed into the medical schools. The students learned the teachings of Hippocrates, which included astrology. Helena excelled and eventually surpassed Heracleus in skill. While in trance, Caldwell, completely absorbed in Helena, delivered lengthy lectures to her long-ago medical students.

The regressions also solved the mysteries of her

nightmare and her familiarity with the works of George Eliot. The nightmare seemed to be a fragment of a life as Sister Maria Theresa, a follower of Fra Girolamo Savonarola, a fifteenth-century Italian Dominican who led an effort to reform the corrupt court of Pope Alexander VI. Savonarola was excommunicated in 1497 and was burned at the stake a year later as a false prophet. According to Caldwell, Maria Theresa was denounced as a witch and heretic and imprisoned in a bell tower in Florence. To escape torture, she threw herself out the tower window to her death.

Although Caldwell had exhibited startling familiarity with the works of Eliot, she had not lived before as the famous writer. According to her recall, delivered in an Irish brogue, she was Jeannie McGill, Eliot's Irish chambermaid. McGill had been put out to work at age ten and was eventually taken in by Eliot. She worked for the writer for three years, until a woman in the household accused her of stealing a ring, and McGill was turned over to the police. She was sent to a workhouse, where she hanged herself.

Caldwell recalled other lives in Atlantis, Lemuria, Egypt, Peru, China, France, and Mexico—she had thirty-seven lives in all, according to a psychic reader. In most of them, she was poor and abused, and forever cold and miserable. In her last life before that of Caldwell, she had been Wilma Sims, a blue-eyed, flaxen-haired girl born in a Battersea workhouse. Sims had died in 1898, two years before Caldwell was born. Throughout her current life, Caldwell had a great fear of poverty, and often felt wretched, depressed, and abused.

Weaving through her many lives was an ongoing love triangle of cosmic proportions. The unseen presence who aided Caldwell in her work was identified as the Lord Darios, archangel of the planet Melina, which was ruled by his brother, Lucifer. Darios had taken

Caldwell as his bride when she was fifteen and was living by the seashore on the legendary lost continent of Lemuria. She described Lemuria as almost a Garden of Eden, a land in which there was no disease and people lived to be 600 years old or more before they died. One night as she was alone in her garden, watching the moon rise, Darios appeared to her, a brilliant being with rays of light streaming from him. She thought he was God and worshiped him. He told her he had seen her many times and wanted her for his bride. He then transported her to another plane of reality to Melina, where they were married.

Though she loved Darios, she was lonely most of the time, isolated in a huge white palace protected on one side by a bottomless black chasm. She fell in love with another man, Estanbul, one of her tutors. Jealous, Darios exiled Estanbul from Melina. There followed Caldwell's many lives on Earth, in which she searched for Estanbul, hoping to redeem him with her love so that he could return to Melina. She found him over and over again (he had been Savonarola, for example), but never gained his love; she was constantly thwarted by the invisible presence of Darios. At last she met Estanbul in the form of Marcus Reback. The two enjoyed a soul-mate marriage for more than forty years. Between lives, Caldwell said, her spirit always returned to Melina.

In her book *Dialogues with the Devil*, an exchange between Lucifer and the archangel Michael, Caldwell wrote about the planet Melina, which was destroyed by God out of displeasure. Under hypnosis, Caldwell said Earth was in danger of being destroyed because of the corruption and greed of its inhabitants, and that Darios had laughed at the puny efforts of Christ to sacrifice himself to try to save the planet.

When shown the transcripts of her regressions, Caldwell could scarcely believe them. They failed to convince her of the existence of reincarnation. Her own life, she said, had been filled with despair, and she could imagine nothing worse than having to come back and live again. Caldwell died in 1985. Perhaps she has gone once again to meet her jealous lover, Lord Darios.

CHAPTER FOURTEEN

Marion Zimmer Bradley's Mirror of the Past

Marion Zimmer Bradley, best-selling author of science fiction, fantasy, and historical novels, believes in the possibility of reincarnation and has made use of some of her own past-life memories in her works. Her recalled lives include those of a Spanish soldier and a male cowherd in Scandinavia in the thirteenth or fourteenth century, as well as others that she discusses here. The past lives that have been particularly meaningful to her work as a writer deal with pagan religions and mysteries, goddess worship, and magic. One of her most popular works, *The Mists of Avalon*, retells the story of King Arthur from the viewpoints of the women around him, including the central character, Morgaine (Morgan Le Fay), priestess of the Goddess and the Mysteries, who spent seven years learning the magical arts from Viviane, the Lady of the Lake. *The Firebrand* concerns the fall of Troy, as seen through the eyes of Kassandra (Cassandra), prophetess and priestess. Kassandra herself is vaguely aware of having a previous life as a serpent-handling priestess of the Sun Lord.

In her present life, Bradley describes herself an occultist, having had since childhood a strong interest in classical ceremonial magic, the mystery religions, and the Authurian legend. She was for a time a member of the Rosicrucians, as well as various occult groups. She has numerous friends in the Wiccan community, but is not herself a witch, saying that is not her path in this life. She is an ordained priest of the Neo-Catholic Church, a vaguely Theosophical group. Perhaps it is her own past lives as a priestess that help make her characters so compellingly real.

Bradley's past lives have involved her two husbands, Robert Bradley, from whom she separated in 1959 and divorced in 1964 (he died in 1966), and Walter Breen, from whom she was separated in 1979, but with whom she remains close friends. Her awareness of her past lives began surfacing as spontaneous recall when she was in her teens.

I started experiencing them [past lives] more or less on my own. I was about fourteen. You could say it was a form of dissociative reverie. They would go away for a while, and then I'd find myself remembering something else [from the past]. For a long time I thought I was going nuts, and then I realized that this is something that just happens.

When I was sixteen, I almost got killed in an automobile accident. I was crossing the street in front of the school bus and a car came straight at me from the other side. I was hit in the leg. I found myself facing death and I felt a weird resignation. I thought, "Well, that's it, I'm dead. Isn't that strange?" I felt myself flying through the air.

Then I woke up and I picked myself up, rather surprised and disappointed to find that I wasn't dead.

I think it was around that time in my life that I realized, as I said in one of my books, that death is the least final thing in the world. From that time on, I have never had any fear of it. When my daughter, Moira, was born in 1966, my heart stopped and I did die, and I had one of these classic near-death experiences, a meeting with a sort of person who said I wasn't supposed to come yet. Actually, the person said in effect that I could come if I wanted to, but I had the girl I'd always wanted and I didn't think Walter could raise a girl alone. So I went back.

Bradley said she was not shocked by the near-death experience:

When these things happen, you sort of say, "Well, yes, of course," It's hard to put these things into words. They're more impressions. The main things that surprised me were the lights and the music. I got the impression of a tremendous city, you could say a city of light. The one thing I wanted in the world was to join the music and be part of it. The music was . . . well, the nearest I've ever heard to it is a famous piece by Ralph Vaughan Williams called *Fantasia on a Theme by Thomas Tallis* [a medieval churchman], which sounds more like heavenly music than anything I can think of. I always thought I would be cheated if I didn't get to be part of the heavenly choir, because I've always cared so much about singing. I'll be perfectly happy if they give me a harp and tell me to play it.

Bradley used her near-death experience in two of her books, *In the Steps of the Master* and *The Firebrand;* the latter includes a description faithful to what Bradley encountered herself. In *The Firebrand,* Kassandra, priestess in Troy's temple of Apollo the Sun Lord, comes to the threshold of death. In the fall of Troy, she is raped and nearly killed by an enemy soldier. She feels herself leave her pain-racked body, rise, and move over a flat, featureless, gray plain that is and is not the city of Troy. It is the plain of the dead, and she sees others who are dead, some of them confused soldiers. The dead include Priam, her father; Penthesilea, the Amazon queen who raised Kassandra and taught her many skills and who was slain by Akhilles (Achilles); and the handsome Khryse, a priest in Kassandra's temple. When Kassandra sees Penthesilea, smiling and unwounded, she runs into the Amazon's arms and is surprised to find them solid:

Beyond Penthesilea the plain of the dead faded away, and Kassandra could see what looked like blinding light—twice the brilliance of the Sun Lord as she had seen Him in her first overpowering vision; and through the light, she made out the form of a great Temple, larger than the one where she had served in Colchis, and even more beautiful.

She whispered in awe, "Is that where I am to go?"

Beyond the light she began to hear music: harps and other instruments, swelling and filling the air with harmony like a dozen—no, a hundred voices, all joined together in song, clear and high and coming closer. This was what she had thought the Sun Lord's house would be. Khryse was standing in the doorway, beckoning to her; his face was free of the dissatisfaction and greed she had seen in it, so that he was at last what she had always believed him. He held out his arms, and she was ready to run into them. . . .

But Penthesilea was standing in her way—or was it the Warrior Maiden Herself, wearing the armor of the Amazon? . . .

"No," Penthesilea said; "no, Kassandra. Not yet."

Kassandra struggled to form words. It was the place she had seen in her dreams, the place where she had always known she belonged. And not only Khryse, but everyone she had loved was there, awaiting her, waiting for her voice to fill the place open in that great blended choir.

"No." Penthesilea's voice was sorrowful, but inflexible, and she held Kassandra back as one restrains a small child. "You cannot go yet; there is still something you must do among the living. You could not leave with Aeneas; you cannot come with me. You must go back, Kassandra; it is not time for you."

The beautifully molded face under the shining helmet was beginning to break up into a sunburst of brilliant sparkles. Kassandra fought to keep it in focus. "But I want to go . . . the light . . . the music . . ." she said.

The light was fading, and around her was darkness; she was aware of a ghastly smell, like death, like vomit; she was lying on the dirt floor of some kind of rough shelter. *Then I'm not dead after all.* Her only emotion was bitter disappointment. She fought to hold on to the memory of the light, but already it was disappearing. She was conscious of pain in her body. She was bleeding, and part of what she smelled was her own blood on her face and covering her shift. . . .

—Marion Zimmer Bradley,
The Firebrand

Bradley explored her past lives by using a self-induced trance, sometimes in the company of others.

I'm quite certain I have known Walter many times before. I think he's been a musician in many lives. I think he was one of the minor Bachs. There were about forty of them in at least five generations that we know of, most of them somewhere in the sixteenth century. Walter once sat down and played the harpsichord without ever having had piano lessons, as though he'd belonged to it all of his life. He picked up a harp one day and just played it.

I remember being a sort of official in the Roman Empire under Tiberius. Walter was my adopted son. He was Greek. We're still always arguing about the Romans and the Greeks. We make jokes and say it's a habit we've kept up for nineteen hundred years. I think I met Tiberius once. He seems to have been very much of a tough guy. I was at that time some sort of army official, an inspector of military camps. I died when a house collapsed on top of me. It was in a slum someplace. I'd gone there to inspect it and it collapsed.

When I went to England in 1978, I visited some of the Roman sites and found them very interesting. Sprague de Camp, who was very much an archaeologist, said that there couldn't have been cavalry in the Roman times because they hadn't invented the stirrup to control the horses. I know [from this past life] that they did, because they had Parthian archers who were cavalry. Sprague said no one has ever found irons for the stirrups. I seem to remember that the stirrups had been made of leather in those days.

I did at one time know my name in that life, but I don't remember it now. I remember seeing an inscription with my name on it. It was something like Lucius Valerius. I can't be exact about it. I saw a tombstone of one of my family, I think, in a book Walter had of Roman inscriptions.

Bradley says her past lives may have included that of Charlotte Brontë (1816–55), the English novelist and poet whose novels include *Jane Eyre, Shirley,* and *Villette* and whose lyric poems are considered to be among the best in English poetry.

I have a feeling that I might have been Charlotte Brontë because I understand a lot of things about her that other people don't. I seem to understand about how she felt about Branwell, her brother, who was a drunk. She said in one of her letters that she had suffered a great deal with him, seeing a man whom she loved and respected deteriorate into the worst sort of person. I can relate to that because the same thing happened to my father, of whom I was extremely fond.

Two or three times, I've had past-life flashes about Charlotte. I thought I heard someone calling to me on one occasion. I later discovered what I didn't know then, that "Talli" was one of her nicknames, and I thought I'd heard someone calling me by that name. She'd evidently been called that as a small child.

There was a poem that I kept seeing in my mind's eye, and I thought it was Emily Brontë's. I went all through her work [but couldn't find it]. Then it flashed in my mind that it might have been one of those that Charlotte burned after Emily died—she burned everything she found because she knew that Emily did not want them printed. I used the poem at the end of my book *Darkover Landfall*.

Asked if she has felt any influence from Charlotte Brontë upon her writing, Bradley made this observation:

I have been very meticulous about emotions. If emotions are true, that is much more important than anything else. My late friend Theodore Sturgeon said that writing is the telling of passionate emotional relationships. I've always felt that way. She [Charlotte] seems to have, too. From reading her letters, one would assume that it was the most important thing in her life.

Although I believe in reincarnation, I also disbelieve it. I am not emotionally committed to the idea. I like believing that it might have been true, because Charlotte is, after all, somebody I admire tremendously. But I am definitely not one of these people who get their teeth into a theory and hang on to it for dear life.

Bradley, who was born in 1930, said her most recent past life took place around the turn of the twentieth century.

During the First World War, I was a young kid in school in Belgium someplace. I seemed to have known Walter then. And I seem to have from that life a series of very strange memories of being between lives. I remember that I died in bombing [of my school] in the First World War around 1913 or 1914. I was a boy [Marty] about seventeen years old. As I was dying, I saw the kid whom I think was Walter—his name was Teddy—standing outside the door waiting for me. I said, "Is Teddy all right?" And the school people were telling me, "Oh, yes, he's fine." But I knew that he'd been killed in the bombing, and that I would probably die very soon, and I did. The stranger thing is, I think I died by accident, that I should have lived and been part of that Edwardian scene. Brad [Robert Bradley] actually fought in World War I—he was in France.

Once or twice, looking in a mirror, I have seen Marty. I'll be looking in a mirror and suddenly my face will dissolve and I will see his face looking out at me. It's very much a masculine face and not at all like mine. I would say it has very sharp features, very slender and very blond.

In the between-lives period, I seem to have realized what I was meant to do in this life. My purpose is to pick up people who have left the path and who are into terribly materialistic things. That's the reason I write fantastic stuff—but almost all of fantasy is based on Hermetic philosophy. If I can convince [materialistic people] that I believe in these things, and I'm obviously not crazy, then they can believe them, too, and not be thought crazy.

This is why I've been shoved into science fiction. Every time I've tried to get out of it, to write straightforward books, I've been shoved back in. I remember once a teacher asked me why I wasted my mind on something like this. I said, "Oh, you think it's better to write stories about adultery in the suburbs?" At least in science fiction, you're thinking about the future. Science fiction is a basic sort of affirmation, in a way, that there will be a future, that the human race will survive.

I've used [what it's like in the between lives] several times in the Darkover books. There's something I call the Overworld, which I think resembles the astral planes. In that world you present the visual image as you think of yourself. For instance, one man in my books realized that his wife and his wife's sister weren't really identical twins because they looked different in that world. Also, you can be where you want to be with the speed of light.

In the late 1960s, Bradley's dissociative reveries of past-life memories began to interfere with her waking consciousness, and she made an effort to suppress them.

Around 1967 or so, I discovered that I was having these [reveries] and they were something like focal seizures. I would get wound into them and it would seem that everything was happening in slow motion very far off. I'd find myself not able to cope with the outside world. I decided this wasn't doing me any good. [When it happened] I would stop thinking about it and turn my attention very quickly away so that I wouldn't get caught up in these things. I got to where I stopped them. Now they're just flashes.

I have taken LSD a few times [mostly between 1965 and 1969]. I can't anymore because it lowers my blood sugar too much—I am diabetic. I don't think it [had anything to do with past-life recall]. It's true that the central vision of *The Mists of Avalon* came from it. The last time I took LSD was when I started working on *Mists*. That was in 1978. By then I had tapered off to taking it about once a year as a sort of religious experience, the sort of thing where you take two days to prepare, one day to take it, and two days to integrate the insights from it. There was never any case of taking it just for fun. I'd read a lot about its use in psychology [when] it was not illegal.

The flood of ideas that I got coalesced into the central vision [of *Mists*]. I focused on the training of the priestesses, which was another of my past lives. I think I have always been a priestess, through most of prehistory and up until about the fourth century. In the early days most women did nothing but sit around and spin. Priestesses were entrusted with almost all the medical knowledge and timekeeping. I wrote a lot about that in *The Firebrand*.

Bradley has had past-life memories involving her first husband, Robert Bradley. However, Brad, as he was called, didn't take them very seriously. His wife portrayed him (to his annoyance) in two of her works: as Frobisher in the short story "Hero's Moon" and as Riveda in the novel *The Fall of Atlantis*. None of her past-life recollections involving Walter have shed light on why she and he have met time and time again.

I have sometimes thought of this Platonics idea . . . that the real thing is complete in some other basic world, and in this world we're just trying to attain it as if it were there in perfect form. Here in this world we get a dim echo of it. This is the true theory of "archetypes."

CHAPTER FIFTEEN

Lessons and Missions

Looking at past lives often fosters growth. As Cayce noted, every soul reincarnates with a specific agenda of karmic lessons to learn and debts to repay. Sometimes, in the course of a life, we lose sight of that agenda, and so need to reincarnate yet again. By examining past lives, one can see the reasons for present situations and relationships as well as the patterns of behavior and mistakes. In many cases, we may have been presented with repeated opportunities for a particular balancing of karma, yet ignored or missed them. Knowledge gleaned from past lives, then, can quicken karmic growth by keeping us on the right track.

Past lives also can bring us a greater understanding of who we are. The memories that surface, no matter what the method, rise up for a reason: to teach us about ourselves. We watch our tragedies and triumphs, failures and successes, strengths and weaknesses. It is then up to us to put the information to good use.

To Know Thyself

Laurie McQuary has extensively explored some of her past lives and has learned a great deal about herself. Most of her information surfaces spontaneously through intuition and what she calls a "cognizant knowing," which enables her to tune in to the past. She also has obtained past-life information from her dreams, from consultations with other psychics and regressionists, and from her own readings for others.

Earlier in her present life, McQuary felt she was always on the run—from abusive relationships and financial hardship. Past lives helped her put those circumstances in perspective and break negative patterns so that she could become stronger and whole. In addition, she discovered, or rediscovered, her deep feeling of kinship with Native Americans. She talked about some of her past-life recollections:

As early as eighteen, I recognized I was on my own trying to figure out where I belonged in life. I investigated up to eight religions, trying to find one where I fit. I never found anything until I discovered the Spiritualist Church, which is quite a believer in reincarnation. This was twenty-six or twenty-seven years ago, and reincarnation was not a big fad then—people didn't talk about it and I had never heard about it. But the moment I heard the theory, it felt right. I knew there had to be some explanation for everything I'd gone through by eighteen.

I've had a problem with men in my life, being mistreated mentally and physically from the time I was little. I was always trying to understand why. I was sexually abused as a small child by my stepfather, whom I believed was my father. I was only two when my mother married him, and he died of cancer when I was seven. The day he died, she told me he wasn't my father.

I had other incidents of abuse from strangers, until I was eleven or twelve. Then my mother remarried for the third time, and that man beat me until I was eighteen. In his past lifetimes, I always see him as an inquisitor and a judge. I'm sure I've met him before. Any time you have strong feelings about someone, either good or bad, you can bet it's from a past life.

As I began to tap into past lives, I realized that I had several lifetimes as a man who abused women. In one life, for example, I was a man in Spain, and worked for a circus or traveling show. I beat women. I was just horrible, and I ended up getting hung.

What better way to understand what it's like to be abused than to come back as an abused woman myself? After suffering childhood abuse, I then had a tendency to be drawn to the same type of man that I was in that Spanish life, sort of the self-made, off-the-wall, risqué, irresponsible woman-hater. My second husband shot at me once with a .45. The bullet missed, went through the wall, and hit the bed of the people next door.

Once I accepted what reincarnation meant, then it began to make sense to me why I've felt so attracted to certain cultures and so repelled by others. One culture in particular that mystified me for years was that of the Orient. Aside from not liking Chinese food, I even had an aversion to Chinese people. I didn't know why I didn't like them, I just felt turned off.

I had a dream that led to an explanation for this. In the dream, I was in the Orient and was standing next to an ox cart where there was a little, fat baby boy sitting on straw. He was naked. It was apparently summertime. I was terribly upset, crying and crying. The dream was lucid, so I was able to look at myself and say, "That was me in a past life." The reason I was so upset was that we—the boy and I—were traveling more than 200 miles over the mountains because we had been forced to flee our homes. When I woke up, I realized the Orient had never appealed to me because of that unhappy experience in that lifetime. I have always hated making a home move, yet I recently made my seventy-fifth move in twenty-eight years. Obviously, it is a lesson for me to learn how to cope with moving.

I got more information about my negative feelings about the Orient from a friend who did dream reincarnations for others. She was in her eighties. You would ask her for information, and she would come up with reams of paperwork about where you were and what you did. The dreams she dreamed about me in the Orient concerned another life in which I was a well-to-do physician's wife. I'm not sure of the century. My name was something equivalent to "Orange Blossom," and I had long, long black hair that was braided and coiled on top of my head with shells and ornaments. I went through the streets of China delivering my husband's medicinal herbs. I was dressed in black silk pants and an embroidered jacket done in pinks and oranges. The jacket had an elongated neck and long sleeves. I wore a lot of bracelets that were hidden up inside the sleeves. For some reason, I carried some jewels sewn into the inside of the coat.

I was kidnapped and held for ransom by bandits from the mountains. From the way I was dressed and the jewelry I wore, and possibly because of the little ricksha I was traveling in, they could ascertain that I had money. They found out who my husband was, but for some reason, it never came about that he was able to rescue me. I was taken to the mountains to live with these people, and I never got to go home.

While I was in the mountains, I became pregnant and had a child. When she was about six, we ran away, but got lost and starved to death in the mountains. She is the daughter I have in this lifetime [Kirsten]. We've been alone together a lot in this life. I lost her father [McQuary's first husband] when she was five months old, and we experienced the same feeling of survival from that past life. Also in this lifetime, I had a deep-seated anxiety that bordered on fear about getting home before dark, especially in the wintertime. I feel it was connected to that kidnapping.

Another past life of hardship and desperation involved McQuary's son, Scott, from her second marriage.

It was back in ancient times in the Middle East, and we were very poor. I had several children and the boy who was Scott was my oldest child. To make ends meet, I sent him out to beg. So that he would be more pitiful to people, I maimed him on purpose, by scarring his face with a piece of burning wood. When I flashed on this, it nearly killed me. It brought tears to my face. I told Scott about it. He's very psychic and has tremendous past-life dreams about himself. This struck chords with both of us.

In the present life, things were really hard financially for us for years. I was divorced from my second husband for seven years and it was nothing but hard times. The emotions, and sometimes the circumstances, will be the same as what you've gone through in another lifetime.

In one of the many lives she recalls, McQuary remembers again running from trouble.

I was in Spain around the sixteenth century. My second husband from this life was a priest in that one, and I was an important lady and had money. There was some kind of war or upset going on, and I had great fear for my land, my money, and my life. The priest sheltered me by taking me into a monastery or abbey. He was like a mentor and taught me a lot.

Also during that life, McQuary said, she abused horses, a karmic debt that led, ironically, to the flowering of her psychic talent in the present. When she was eighteen, she was bucked off a horse, struck her head, and lapsed into a coma for three weeks. A few months after she regained consciousness, she began having precognitive dreams and experiencing telepathy. The experience initially frightened her, but she eventually accepted her new ability and learned how to control and use it.

McQuary said that in a subsequent life, about 200 years after the life in sixteenth-century Spain, she was a working-class woman who ran away from responsibility:

I was a curly-haired blonde in eighteenth-century England. I wore a white dress with a corset and bodice. I was probably nothing more than a call girl, and I had absolutely no responsibilities in life. All I wanted to do was party. I saw myself playing on this hillside. There was another woman and we were just having a high old time, drinking and running around. I knew that this is why I now have a problem with women who are totally irresponsible and misuse their sexuality.

While some past lives have explained to McQuary her aversions and difficulties, others have revealed the reason for her lifelong identification with Native Americans, particularly the Apache of the Southwest and also the Cherokee and Sioux. When she participated in shamanic workshops, she immediately found herself transported back in time about 100 to 200 years. Her affinity with Native Americans is so strong that she has decided to relocate to the Southwest, a move that for her will be "going home":

From the time I was about seven, I would tell total strangers that I was an Apache. My parents probably thought I needed a psychiatrist! We lived in Cleveland, Ohio, and we had nothing to do with Indians, but I was absolutely convinced that I was part Indian. In the eighth grade, I once got up in social studies class, furious because my teacher said the Indians were "savages." I had never read anything about them, but I gave a discourse in class on the Indians, what their society was like and that they were not savages, but had rules to live by. The whole class laughed at me.

All through my growing-up years I continued to be fascinated with American Indians. I read all I could about them. When I was about fifteen, I decided that one day I would live on an Indian reservation. When I was thirty-four, I went to live on the Warm Springs reservation [in Oregon]. My husband at the time was hired as the drug and alcohol counselor there, and I was a nurse. I lived there for a year and a half, and I loved it. It certainly didn't happen by design. I think I had to complete that part of myself. While I was there, I often was asked if I was part Indian. I find that many times if you have a particular lifetime that you're still tied to, you will reflect that look no matter what your nationality is in this lifetime.

Through past-life recall, McQuary discovered that she has had numerous lives as a Native American, including one in which she and Scott were husband and wife. In another American Indian life, she was a young woman with an unusual occupation.

I was probably Sioux, in the North Plains. I was very different for that time in that I didn't want a man in my life. I wanted to be left alone and free. I became a runner for my tribe, carrying messages to and from other tribes. The Indians did allow people their individuality. I probably wasn't totally accepted by everyone, but I was given other accolades and told I could do certain things and be my own person. I saw myself running and getting lost, and having a bad fall in a crevasse, where I died. I was probably in my twenties. There also seems to have been a thwarted love affair, a young man in my tribe who loved me. I cared about him, but I needed to reject him.

McQuary also remembers several past lives in ancient Egypt, another culture to which she feels a strong connection. She believes she may have been the only female pharaoh, Hatshepsut, who ruled in the Eighteenth Dynasty of the New Kingdom, from about 1506 B.C. until her death in 1482 B.C. When Pharaoh Thutmose II died in 1504, he had no male heirs by

Hatshepsut, who was his major queen. The throne was passed to Thutmose III, a ten-year-old boy by a minor wife, and Hatshepsut was named regent. In the second year of Thutmose III's regency, Hatshepsut boldly took the kingship herself and became the dominant ruler. She pursued a pacifist policy during her reign. Much of her statuary and relief art depicts her as male. When Thutmose III assumed sole rule upon her death, he launched a more aggressive, warlike policy. Later in his reign, an effort was made to erase the memory and defile the name of Hatshepsut. McQuary first learned about her from a book by Barbara Corcoran, *Child of the Morning*.

When I started reading it, the descriptions of her felt very, very familiar, especially the one of her as a child and the way she started to grow into a young woman. I felt there was every possibility that I might have been her. She was a pharaoh at sixteen and ruled very well.

The running theme has emerged in various ways in McQuary's past lives, but usually with a stressful or unhappy end. She fled her home in the Orient with the infant boy, ran away from her kidnappers in China, fled her troubles in Spain by taking shelter in a monastery, and ran away from responsibility as an English prostitute. Her unorthodox occupation as a female Native American runner allowed her to run emotionally from a young suitor. McQuary applied her insights from these experiences to her present relationships:

The lesson is certainly not to get into destructive relationships to begin with, but if you are in one, you don't run from it, you learn from it and work it out before you move on.

I recently remarried [for the third time] and

now I have a marvelous husband. I know I knew him in the 1800s in the early West, perhaps in southern California or parts of Nevada. I was an Indian [perhaps Apache] and he was a trapper. He still has a love for everything about the Old West. He's from Reno, Nevada, so that's probably part of it, but I can picture him in that past life. He even looks the part of a trapper: he has a beard and a rugged appearance.

McQuary said she has had more lives as a man than as a woman, yet her lessons have come primarily from her female lifetimes, including the present. From them she has learned about the use and abuse of power, and about taking responsibility.

This lifetime is the one that I've learned the most from about being a woman, and being a complete woman. I think what women need is recognition without sacrifice and love without compromise. It's taken me all of these lifetimes to learn that and, in this lifetime, to stand up to it. I've learned how to be a man, but I never learned how to be a woman. That's the gift of being able to see my past lives.

The lessons for me are to stand up and be my own person and not be afraid of my own power, which involves the ability see myself through my own eyes, not someone else's eyes; also, to tap into my male side in order to be a strong, assertive female, not aggressive. Everyone has male and female energies, and needs to balance the two.

EMPTY MATERIALISM

One of Ian Stevenson's cases concerns a young man who learned, from remembering his previous life, that indulging oneself in possessions and sensual pleasure does not bring happiness.

In turn–of–the–century India, Laxmi Narain was an arrogant young man with a taste for beautiful women, good food and liquor, and expensive silk clothing. As a wealthy member of the Kayastha caste in Pilibhit, he devoted himself to spending his money in pursuit of these pleasures. He didn't need to work. The inheritance left by his father, Har Narain, spared him that drudgery. He quarreled with his relatives over family property, sued for it, and won, and continued to live in fine style.

Narain was not without some redeeming qualities, however. He gave much money and food to the poor. He was devoutly religious, though he had a strange way of worshiping. At the start of every month, he sequestered himself in the shrine room of his house for ten to fifteen days, meditating and praying, and took all his meals there. The rest of the month, he threw fabulous parties with great feasts of meat, rohu fish, and wine, accompanied by dancing girls and much singing. Narain often played the tabla, a kind of drum that requires a great deal of discipline. He also liked to fly kites with a neighbor friend, Sunder Lal.

As a child, Narain had recalled a previous life as a rajah's son. It was never verified, as his parents were fearful of harmful publicity. He never applied himself to his studies, and lagged far behind his classmates. By age seventeen or eighteen, he had completed the studies of a twelve-year-old. He dropped out of school when his father died.

Though Narain had many women, his favorite was a prostitute named Padma, whom he considered exclusively his. Padma did not share this enthusiasm. One day, Narain spied another man coming out of her apartment, and exploded in rage. He grabbed a gun that his servant always carried, raced up to the rival, and shot him dead.

Narain fled to the sanctuary of his house, where he isolated himself. Because of his money and influence, he got away with the crime. He felt it would be best to move, so he did, to Shajahanpur. He felt no remorse about killing his rival, and was happy not to have been held accountable for it.

But the law of karma was about to catch up with him.

In 1918, not long after his crime, Narain fell ill with fever and lung trouble. He suffered for five months and died on December 15 of that year, at the age of thirty-two. His freewheeling, rich days were over—for a lifetime, at least.

Bishen Chand was four years old when his father, B. Ram Ghulam Kapoor, took him and his older brother to a wedding party in Golda, India. They traveled by train from their home in Bareilly. On the return trip, the train stopped in Pilibhit, which is about fifty kilometers from Bareilly. Much to the surprise of his father, Bishen Chand demanded to get off there, saying he used to live in Pilibhit. His father denied his request, and Bishen Chand cried all the way home.

Bishen Chand had been born on February 7, 1921, and from the age of ten months, he had muttered about "Pilvit" or "Pilivit." As he grew older and learned more words, he said he had lived before as Laxmi Narain. He had an "uncle" named Har Narain. His family ignored his talk, out of superstition that children who speak of previous lives will die early.

B. Ram Ghulam worked as a railway clerk and barely managed to support his family. They were members of the Khsatriya caste, much lower than the caste to which Laxmi Narain had belonged. They were vegetarians and drank no alcohol.

This lifestyle did not suit little Bishen Chand at all. He criticized his father for being poor and thus unable to build a house. He ripped off his cheap cotton clothes and demanded silk garments. Without being taught, he skillfully played the tabla. Around the age of five, he began to demand to eat meat and drink alcohol. He told his parents that even his servants would not eat the vegetarian food served in the house. When he couldn't get meat at home, he visited neighbors and ate it in secret. Once his family bought some brandy for medicinal use. It began "evaporating," and Bishen Chand's sister caught him drinking it. The haughty boy said he was used to drinking.

At about the same time, Bishen Chand astonished his father by asking him why the older man did not keep a mistress, for she would give him great pleasure. He could enjoy the fragrance of her hair and find solace her company, Bishen Chand said.

Word of Bishen Chand reached K. K. N. Sahay, a lawyer who was investigating the past-life memories of his own son. Sahay visited Bishen Chand and persuaded the boy's father to let him verify the story. He recorded twenty-one statements about the life of Laxmi Narain as recalled by Bishen Chand.

In August of 1926, Sahay took Bishen Chand on two visits to Pilibhit. The boy did not recognize his old school—not surprising, in view of Laxmi Narain's attitude toward education—but did recognize the ruins of his former home. Narain had spent so much of his inheritance that, after his death, his mother and relatives were destitute and had allowed the house to disintegrate into a pile of bricks and mud. Significantly, Bishen Chand knew the layout of the intact house and pointed to the correct spot where the staircase had been located. He cried over the ruins and the fact that the house had not been maintained.

He was handed a photograph of Har Narain and

Laxmi Narain, and he correctly identified who was who.

The Pilibhit police superintendent casually asked Bishen Chand to tell about Laxmi Narain's wife and children. The boy replied in the first person, saying he had no children because he had been too steeped in wine and women to consider marrying.

Bishen Chand made a total of forty-eight statements about Laxmi Narain, and nearly all were correct. Only two were completely incorrect: Bishen Chand's identification of Har Narain as his former uncle, and his assertion that Laxmi Narain had died at age twenty, instead of thirty-two.

Bishen Chand showed a great of affection to Laxmi Narain's mother, preferring her to his own. He even implored his father to allow his former mother to live with them; however, to his sorrow, she moved to another town.

He remembered the murder of Narain's rival very clearly, and spoke of it often to his siblings. Like Laxmi Narain, he felt no remorse over it. He had a bad temper and was quarrelsome with some of Laxmi Narain's relatives—perhaps a holdover from the old lawsuit.

Unlike Laxmi Narain, he never showed an interest in kite flying. But he did recognize the gate of his late friend, Sunder Lal.

Padma came to visit when the boy was about six. He still carried a torch for her, but she pointed out to him that he was but a small child while she was "old" (probably in her mid-thirties).

By age seven, the only memories Bishen Chand retained of Laxmi Narain were the murder and his attachment to Padma. He quit playing the tabla at age eight, and gradually accepted the poverty of his family, which relegated him to cheap cotton clothes. He completed his education and went to work for the government, earning a meager living as an excise officer.

In 1944, Bishen Chand saw Padma again by accident. He recognized her, even though she was by now about fifty-two and he had not seen her for nearly twenty years. He hugged her and fainted. That night, he bought a bottle of wine and went to her house. She threw him out and told him to go away. "You lost everything in your previous life," she said. "Now you want to lose everything again."

Two years later, at age twenty-five, Bishen Chand married a girl who, like his parents, was vegetarian and would allow no meat or fish in the house. His small income limited them to simple clothes and a modest lifestyle; he felt he should be giving away money to help others, but had no money to give. His existence was a far cry from the exotic, luxurious life of Laxmi Narain, and it made him feel bitter.

To his credit, he changed over time. Stevenson visited with Bishen Chand in 1969, when he was forty-eight. He still remembered the murder in vivid detail. He felt he had learned from his experiences. He reflected that he was now suffering poverty because of his spoiled behavior and the murder he'd committed in his previous life.

Stevenson observed that Bishen Chand was a person "who had learned that material goods and carnal pleasures do not bring happiness." In his next life, were he to have one, Bishen Chand said he desired not wealth but superior intelligence and mental qualities that would help him achieve something of significance.

Unfinished Business

Some persons are born with an innate sense of purpose; others find it. In either case, past-life recall can sharpen one's focus or steer one back on track.

Kerry (a pseudonym) is a West Coast writer with a lifelong interest in metaphysics and the occult. As she grew older, she began to feel the influence of past lives.

From the time I was small, I've been a compulsive writer. As a kid, I wrote stories, even little books, which I wrote out by hand or typed on this old typewriter and then bound in cardboard. Most of all, I was a recorder of sorts. I had journals and record books on all kinds of subjects. I started neighborhood and school newspapers. I was fascinated by mythology, especially classical mythology.

I also felt very old, even when I was a child. I once wrote in one of my diaries that I felt like "an old, old woman who's cried a thousand times a thousand tears and lived a thousand lives a thousand years." That's a little nonsensical, but I think I was tapping into the feeling of having lived many lives. I've believed in reincarnation for a long time. When I was a teenager, I rejected Christian teachings about one life on earth and then heaven or hell for eternity. It made no sense, especially in light of the incredible inequities of life experienced on this planet.

I feel it's important to use my abilities as a writer to spread knowledge about the hidden side of things. In my research, I feel like I've clicked into things that I've known before. Sometimes I feel like a hollow straw, drawing up stuff from some unknown reservoir. I feel guided. There's this presence around me, a being I perceive as female. I have seen her in dreams. There are others as well, but she seems to be the key one.

I went through a past-life regression once to see if I could find out the sources of my writing ability and sense of purpose. It was a light hypnosis. Even though I believe in reincarnation, I was a little skeptical about really seeing a past life and not something conjured up out of my imagination. Out of all the things I might have imagined, what I saw wasn't any of them.

When I stepped out of the tunnel, I found myself in some town or village that seemed to be medieval. The streets were very narrow. I was surprised at who I was—I was a man, small, thin, and homely. I had a big nose and close-set, almost beady eyes. Everything about me was plain— plain brown hair, plain brown clothes, a sort of tunic outfit with brown shoes. Very drab. I knew I lived alone. It came to me that I was some sort of tradesman. I could see myself delivering big bundles that I carried on my shoulder to monks who lived in a monastery. I saw things in little vignettes, almost like freeze frames, except there was motion within the frame. It was like looking at a series of snapshots that became animated.

Everything about me, who I was and what I did for a living, felt small and unimportant, but some- how I had gotten an education. There was no explanation given as to how a lowly tradesman came to be educated. Anyway, I saw myself at- tending a lecture, sitting on a small bench listening to a learned man talk. I don't know who he was, but he was a Paracelsus type, an alchemist. I was very absorbed in what he had to say. I had the feeling I went to lectures often. It came to me that I was convinced that "the monks had gotten it all wrong" about certain spiritual truths.

Then I jumped to the next frame, where I saw myself sitting in my little room—I think I lived over a tavern or something—I was on a wooden bench at a table, and I was writing on paper. It was difficult for me. I felt I was writing the truth, recording it, preserving it. I had no idea what would happen to the writings, but whether or not they would ever be published was not the point. In the regression, I could see my iridescent spirit guide standing over me while I labored away, like she was showing me this scene in particular.

All of a sudden I felt a sharp pain in my right eye, and it almost jarred me out of the regression. It was like a nail or needle was being stabbed straight through it, and I lost the picture of me sitting there writing. I said, ''Oh, the monks have ruined my eye!'' It came to me in a flash that my writings had been discovered and I had been tortured for heresy. Probably killed, but I didn't see my death. I was so unprepared for this that I did not go back into [the regression] to find out.

What hit home for me was that when I was about eight [in the present life], it was discovered that I suffered from amblyopia in my right eye. It's where the eye muscles are weak, which results in ''lazy eye.'' The eye is nearsighted and sometimes turns inward to become cross-eyed. I wasn't cross-eyed, but my right eye was extremely nearsighted, while I had perfect vision in my left eye. For years, I wore glasses with plain glass in the left eye. When I switched to contacts, I only had to wear one, in my right eye. When I got into my twenties, my left eye began to go nearsighted, but my right eye is still far worse. I haven't thought about the amblyopia in years. It struck me that this condition is a lingering trace of that past life.

I feel I am writing now what I didn't finish then, drawing up material from that and other past lives in which I was a keeper of knowledge. I have a sense that I have had several past lives where I have been involved in arcane arts and knowledge, and in ritual. In this life I am spreading the same knowledge in a different way, through books and articles. It's my theory that many people who are involved in the New Age area—and I'm not talking about the fads—had past lives in which they were holy men and women, healers, magicians, and the like. They have reincarnated in the present to help others reunite with spirit. That's one of the main reasons I'm here.

CHAPTER SIXTEEN

A Pagan Priestess Finds
Her Roots

From an early age, Selena Fox has had a sense of mission, a distinct feeling that she is here to help make some changes for the better on Planet Earth. Her mission has manifested itself in the form of a planetary healing ministry and Circle Sanctuary, a Wiccan church located on a nature preserve and herb farm between Mount Horeb and Barneveld in Wisconsin. Circle Sanctuary focuses on communion with the divine through nature. As high priestess of Circle, Fox, along with her husband, Dennis Carpenter, directs a wide range of spiritual, environmental, healing, personal growth, and networking activities for national and international nature religious groups. She also devotes much effort to defending religious freedom rights for Wiccans and Pagans.

To meet Fox is to be touched by a warm and loving presence. "Earth mother" is a term that springs to mind. She is deeply connected to nature, and radiates an aura of harmony with the elemental forces and the psychic vibrations of the planet. She is also deeply connected to the Goddess. Over the years, Fox has come to recognize that her skills, knowledge, and mission in this life have been developed over a series of lifetimes.

My earliest recollection of past-life material came to me as a child, especially during my teen years. I found I had a very strong affinity with ancient Rome, in particular the time of Caesar Augustus. I became immersed in Roman mythology. I had been raised a Southern Baptist, and as I was drawn to the study of classical Latin, it completely surprised my parents. I picked up Latin very easily and won awards in junior high and high school, and I went on to become president of the classics honor society in college. I feel that part of myself in this life is rooted in ancient Rome. In terms of any historical figures I've felt an affinity with, it is Caesar Augustus's daughter, Julia. Whether I was her or just connected with her in some way, I don't know, but I have been intrigued by her ever since I began my studies of ancient Rome.

From childhood, Fox has had psychic and mystical visions, and has experienced out-of-body travel. Such experiences, coupled with her interest in classics, led her to Wicca and Paganism. She conducted her first Pagan ritual at age twenty-one, as president of Eta Sigma Phi, the classics honor society, at the College of William and Mary in Virginia. She graduated cum laude with a bachelor of science degree in psychology. Following college, she was initiated into several Wiccan traditions, which are comparable to denominations in Christianity.

In 1974, not long after moving to Wiconsin, Fox was inspired in a meditation to found Circle Sanctuary. With her partner at the time, Jim Alan, and a group of friends, she formed the beginnings of Circle Sanctuary, which was incorporated as a Wiccan church in 1978. The same year, Fox began to devote herself full-time to her ministry. In 1983, the group purchased a 200-acre nature preserve, where it is presently located.

Despite the growth and success of Circle, and Fox's personal feelings of accomplishment and contribution concerning her mission, the path has been strewn with obstacles. Chief among those are the misconceptions held by non-Pagans, who equate Wicca and Paganism with devil worship—a problem rooted in past lives, Fox has discovered.

Some of Fox's most meaningful past-life information has come to her in dreams. Her past-life dreams are always unusual: highly vivid, intense, often lucid. They occur spontaneously and are harbingers of events to come that enable her to integrate past-life memories or experiences into her present life. The information sheds much light on who she is and her present mission as a Pagan priestess. "Whenever I have a dream like this, which some people would call a lucid dream, or high dream, or big dream, I spend considerable time in my waking life reflecting as to why I had it and what is the message," Fox said.

She has also experienced past-life recollections in flashbacks. She had a particularly strong flashback in 1986, during a prolonged legal controversy over the zoning of the Circle Sanctuary land, an issue that threatened to end Circle's status and operation as a church. When the zoning questions were raised by local government, Fox and Dennis Carpenter were forced to secure legal help, so clouded was the issue by mistaken local belief that Circle was a satanic group. Fox and Carpenter attended numerous hearings and public meetings to set the record straight and defend their rights. The hearings were dubbed "the Witch Trials of Barneveld" in the media. Fox described what happened one night:

I walked into the hearing room, which was packed with people. There was a line of older white men sitting behind a table in the front. Feelings came up within me about me being on trial—being tried as a witch in the Middle Ages. It was a very stressful experience for me. I was interrogated by people in the audience and by government officials, and I did my best to answer their questions about me and my religious practices. It certainly was nothing compared to what went on in the Middle Ages, but I felt myself reliving something that I had been through before. Over the years, I've had dreams about dying as a witch. There were witch trials and intense persecution, and I saw myself being burned.

I think part of the reason I'm such a strong activist for the Wiccan religion is not just because of what has been done to me personally and to Circle Sanctuary as a Wiccan church, but because I feel that I've come back in this life to help revive nature religions.

I also believe some of the knowledge I have about working with herbs and doing meditations with nature are a result of having been a witch in another life, and now that knowledge has come back in this life. I have a very strong affinity with certain plants, such as lemon balm, mint, and mugwort, which I think goes beyond this life. When I am out picking herbs or walking in nature, things come to me intuitively.

The following are Fox's accounts of three startling past-life experiences, all of which began with dreams. The first occurred in the summer of 1973, within a year of her move to Madison, Wisconsin. Fox was unfamiliar with the state and its history and geography; Circle Sanctuary had yet to be born.

I had only been in Madison for a short while. I was enrolled at a technical school, studying commercial art and photography, and I was involved in creative development. I mention this because it is my theory that people who make creative work part of their day-to-day activities are more likely to trigger "peak experiences" within themselves.

One night, I had this very, very vivid dream. I saw myself as a young boy, an adolescent about age twelve, and I was wearing some kind of light-colored, loose garment. It was the summer solstice. I was looking out over a grassy plain at a long, serpentine procession of people. The whole tribe was marching in ceremony, with drumming and chanting, and approaching a gigantic earthen-step pyramid that rose up out of the ground to about twenty feet in height. It was called the Temple of the Sun or the Mound of the Sun. I could see another pyramid mound, the Temple of the Moon, off in the distance, and then another one, the Temple of the Earth. At first, I felt myself as part of the procession. Then I went up to the top of the mound with what appeared to be a priest. There was a fire there—I felt it was an eternal solar fire, kept going all the time—and some kind of altar. I was playing a role in the ceremony, rather like an altar boy. I felt like I was there, yet part of me was watching myself as I was reliving this experience.

I saw myself looking out over the procession.

The sun was high in the sky. The people wore feathered headdresses, not like Plains Indians, but more like Aztecs or Mayas. They had shiny breastplates made out of gold, copper, or some brasslike metal. The breastplates gleamed and glittered in the sun—they were radiant. The chanting stopped. In the silence, offerings were made—herbs were put into the fire, and the incense was very sweet. As the perfume rose in the air, the chanting began again. I looked down at the wave of people. Suddenly I found myself leaving my body in this scene and traveling rapidly through time and space, and then I felt myself back in the present.

It was a lucid dream, almost like an astral projection. I was aware of what was going on; I was even aware that I was dreaming. Throughout it, I was in a very high spiritual state. As I was coming back into my body in the here and now, I felt myself ask, "Where is this place, where is this place?" I had never heard of anything like earthen pyramid mounds existing in Wisconsin. Then, flashing before my mind's eye, I saw a map of Wisconsin, and a forefinger pointing to a spot about midway between Madison and Milwaukee. I saw no other names on the map, just a straight line, like a road, and a finger pointing to this spot. Then I woke up. I was so taken by the experience that the first thing I did before writing the dream down was to get a Wisconsin map. I moved my finger along the map and saw that there was an interstate highway between Madison and Milwaukee. I moved my hand along and came to a point that approximated the point on the map in my dream. I saw the word "Aztalan," and chills ran up and down my spine. I knew that was it. Instant recognition! And I knew I had to visit that place, though I did not own a vehicle at the time and had no transportation.

For the next several weeks, I asked various people about Aztalan. I had been a student of ancient Greek and Roman cultures, but knew practically nothing about ancient Paganism in America. I found out that the spot I'd seen on the map was now a park, but had once been the site of an ancient Indian village and pyramid mounds. It had been known to Indian tribes for centuries, though it had not been settled by tribes native to the area. In fact, it was taboo to the woodlands Indians.

I was part of a mystical group, and a few of us decided to take a field trip to Aztalan. None of us had ever been to the park, but we found it easily, relying on extrasensory perception whenever we hit an unmarked fork in the road. When we arrived, I saw two of the three mounds from my dream and had a feeling of great recognition and excitement. I said, "Here they are! Here they are!" They didn't look exactly like the ones in my dream, but were very similar—things obviously have changed—with the exception that only two of the three mounds exist in the here and now. There were no signs of a village.

I went up to the larger mound, which I recognized as the Temple of the Sun. The Temple of the Moon was the smaller of the two mounds. The Temple of the Earth was not visible—the site was flat and had trees growing on it. The vibrations were very strong. I felt a real sense of bonding with the place, that I had lived there before and had come home. My friends and I spent the day there, recharging our energies from the spiritual vibrations of this place. We had a feast, and then went up to the tops of the mounds and meditated on their mystery. I felt very protective of the place, and still do. I feel there are many mysteries connected with the site that are buried somewhere in my psyche, and over the years I have had a quest to find out more about Aztalan.

I went to the state historical society and talked with a woman who had worked on an archaeological dig there. She told me that there had been a third mound, but her findings concerning it hadn't been published. She seemed amazed that I knew about the third mound.

I found that the site had been discovered by whites in 1835. A man named Nathaniel Hyer named it Aztalan, which means "near water," because it seemed to match a site from an ancient Aztec legend. According to the legend, the Aztecs' homeland, Aztalan, was somewhere far north of Mexico. Hyer believed that they had once lived in Wisconsin, and that the "near water" referred to the Crawfish River in Wisconsin, or to the Great Lakes. A map was drawn of the place in 1855. Hyer and some others tried to preserve the site, but in the late 1800s it was sold for farmland for twenty-two dollars and a lot of it was plowed under. Dirt from the mounds was hauled out to fill potholes in roads, and artifacts were carted out by the truckload. As a white settlement, Aztalan was a bustling community for a while, but the railroad passed it by and it turned into a ghost town. I believe that sacred site was desecrated—a causal effect.

Fortunately, in the 1900s there was a greater awareness about these ancient sites and the need to preserve them. A scientific study was made in 1919, and in 1921, the site was turned into the Aztalan Mound Park and was presented to the Wisconsin Archaeological Society. In 1952, it was made a state park, and the two remaining mounds were restored to as close to their former state as possible. Also, archaeologists believed that the site had once been surrounded by a stockade, and a replica of part of the stockade was erected. The park became a National Historic Landmark in 1964.

Nobody really knows who the original builders of Aztalan were, or why their civilization died. Archaeologists believe it was occupied between about A.D. 1100 and 1300 by a people who were very different from the surrounding woodlands tribes, and who had a much more complex society, closer to that of tribes in the southeastern United States or Mexico. The village seems to have been large, but no burial grounds have been found. The remains of what appears to be an Indian princess were discovered in 1920, in a place that was then named Princess Mound. She had been wrapped in belts of clam or oyster shells.

The pyramids clearly were built for religious ceremonial purposes. Remains of a fire were found on top of "Old Smokey," as archaeologists call the largest one, which I call the Temple of the Sun. That certainly checks out with my dream. The remains of what appear to be three underwater stone pyramids have been found at the bottom of Rock Lake, which is nearby.

Finding this place awakened a deep part of myself, and was a very powerful experience. In subsequent years, I've gone there and taken photographs and meditated. I've tried to bring recognition and honor to the Indians who once were there. Some of the archaeological reports call them cannibals, and I'm really disturbed by that. I don't feel that is accurate at all. There have been other archaeological theories that just haven't felt right to me. But I'm relying on an intuitive sense about the place.

I felt I was guided to Aztalan as a way of connecting with part of my spiritual heritage. At the time, I was becoming more seriously involved in Paganism. I was beginning to allow my intuitive self more of a priority in my day-to-day life. This helped usher me into my Pagan priestess work, as well as help me achieve a balance within my own self. In college, I'd gotten a bachelor of science degree in psychology rather than a bachelor of arts. Part of me is very skeptical and needs to be convinced about experiences that can't be explained logically. This experience made me aware how rich consciousness can be, and how it is possible to get information through our own dreams, imagination, and psyche, as well as through the intellectual route of studying books. The world has a lot more mysteries than it appears. What I also got from this is that there is an inner impulse guiding me along the path of my Pagan priesthood, urging me to look at mystery religions and explore the unknown. Since then, as I have walked on the land here at Circle Sanctuary, I have literally had artifacts rise up out of the land to me, and I have felt a real affinity with Native American ways. At times, I've been told that in rituals, when I'm chanting or doing healing work, I actually look like a Native American. I do have a bit of American Indian blood in me, but I also have a sense that I did live as one at least once previously.

The same year, in December 1973, near the winter solstice, I visited my parents, who at the time were living near Washington, D.C. One night, I had a dream in which I saw myself in this life connecting ceremonial objects and statues of deities, which, it seemed, I had once used in ancient Egypt. The feeling I had in the dream was that I had been a priestess in a temple, or possibly a priest, and that I had once cared for these or similar objects. I had a very strong feeling that I needed to find them, connect with them again. In the dream, I saw myself going through the halls of the Smithsonian's Museum of Natural History, and going down into the basement and through a set of doors. I found these Egyptian objects in the basement. As I held them in my hands, I felt connections with the past resurrecting within myself. I could feel memories and feelings coming from these objects, which rekindled some of the spiritual work I had done at that time, and brought it up into my consciousness.

Upon awakening, I was seized with a very strong impulse to go to the Smithsonian to see if indeed these objects were there. The dream was so vivid, with such clear colors and intense feelings, that I regarded it as a very special dream of guidance. There was some important link in my past that this dream was speaking about.

I was so convinced that the objects were at the Smithsonian that I called up a friend of mine, who has a master's degree in anthropology and was visiting the area at that time. I said, "Let's go to the Egyptian exhibit at the Smithsonian." He said, "What Egyptian exhibit?" There wasn't one at that time! But I *knew* I would find these things there. He agreed to meet me at the museum.

I arrived a little early. I went up to the information desk and asked for the Egyptian exhibit. I was told the museum didn't have one, only a sarcophagus that was on display. I said I was there to see some Egyptian artifacts that I believed were kept in the museum. The woman seemed a little puzzled by that, but called one of the curators of the museum. Evidently somebody was in charge of Egyptian artifacts. It was arranged for me to immediately see this person, which must have been unusual, as I had not gone through the customary protocol of writing in advance to get a pass to a nonpublic area.

My friend arrived, and we met this curator, a very nice, very dignified, tall black man who wore a big gold ankh around his neck and had an air of mystery about him, like an aura of being a guardian priest. He didn't say much, just, "Come with me." It was almost as though he thought I'd been sent. He took us down to the basement of the museum and we went through a pair of doorways—just like I had done in my dream—and into this room where there were cabinets with drawers full of artifacts.

I was allowed to go through the drawers, looking at the artifacts and handling them. After several hours, I hadn't found the things I had seen in my dreams. Then I opened up the last drawer, and there they were! Statues of various Egyptian deities—Osiris, Isis, and Bast, the cat goddess. I was particularly drawn to the cat goddess statues, and there were several of those. Some were about six inches tall and clearly were intended to be put on altars. There were amulets that were a few inches high.

I was so elated. It's hard to put my feelings into words. As I handled these and the other objects, I felt shivers go up and down my spine and surges of electricity go through me. I was so excited—it was so wonderful to reconnect with these objects. I don't know if these were the same objects from another life or only similar, but finding them had a dramatic impact on me spiritually. I felt power coming from the objects and passing into me, as if I had reclaimed a spiritual heritage. A part of me connected with something very, very old, and it seemed to be an aspect of myself, a part of my soul. I felt this in both my body and my heart. My friend was amazed, and we both continued to be in a high spiritual state for the rest of the day, long after we left the museum.

This experience proved to be the turning point in my spiritual leadership work as a priestess in this life. Shortly after this happened, I became a priestess of a ceremonial magic group. I worked with a man, a priest of the group, who was very interested and involved in the study of ancient Egypt. The group itself delved more into the Egyptian mysteries. There was a synchronicity involved, a feeling among all of us that we had been in ancient Egypt together, though I don't know during which dynasty.

Other synchronistic things happened. Once, I was in a shopping mall and had the intuitive urge to go in a bookstore. There I found a statue of Bast, which I purchased and still have to this day. Over the years, I have connected with still other people interested in studying about the ancient Egyptian religion.

In 1986, on Beltane [May Day], I had a dream in which I saw myself in a jungle in the Yucatan questing for the remains of a Mayan temple that I had once served in, in a past life. It was a very short dream that seemed to be in the present, but kept flashing back and forth between the present and the past. The colors were very vivid. The name "Temple of the Jaguar" came to me. Part of the dream seemed symbolic and part of it was like I was actually in the jungle. I love cats, and they have played a very important part in my life as friends and as spiritual symbols.

When I came out of the dream, I knew I needed to find somebody in the Yucatan who was on an archaeological dig and share this dream. I didn't know much about the Maya at all, and I've never been to Mexico in this life, nor had I talked to anybody who was steeped in Mayan mythology.

It just so happened that a friend had recently met some people from Florida who were on a dig in the Yucatan at the time. He told me about them when I shared my experience with him. So I wrote to them and shared the dream. I mailed the letter on the first of May. These people were scheduled to leave the dig on the fifteenth of May. Postal officials told me that my letter could take two to three weeks to get there, and I thought, "Oh, great." I put a rush on it, but they didn't give me much hope for it getting there any faster. Well, it got there in four days! Here's another example of things falling into place and doors opening when a positive spiritual force is in motion. The people on the dig told me they had never gotten a letter so fast. I think there was a divine force at work.

Shortly after my letter arrived, these people uncovered a chamber in a pyramid mound where there was a "jaguar priestess," whose body was found with a jaguar-claw amulet around her neck. I was just elated. I felt the reason I'd had that dream was I had once been connected with this temple, and that the woman whose body was found was a priestess of the Mayan religion. I feel I was closely associated with her and that place.

*　　*　　*

What these past-life dream recollections have in common is that they all involve an aspect of myself that was involved in spiritual work. I don't believe that in every lifetime I was serving in a ministerial capacity. I feel I've had these particular recollections because I am doing ministerial work in this life. One of the reasons I look at the dreams as past-life recollections is that it seems to be the best way of accounting for them and putting them into context with my life in terms of who I am, what I'm doing, and what I'm about.

I don't have dreams like these very often. When they happen, I feel like I've dived into the collective unconscious and the inner workings of my own soul. I don't view reincarnation as a personality that survives from life to life—I view it more as a recycling process. I feel that when one dies, one moves into an energy pool or energy bank, dips into it, merges with the Light, and then reemerges and takes on another life. The soul is more of an impulse that goes from life to life through many different personality types and experiences, as a way of getting a well-rounded education.

CHAPTER SEVENTEEN

The Healer Within

Edgar Cayce once said that the ability to heal is both a gift and a talent developed in past lives. All of us seem to possess the gift to some extent, and can develop healing skill by training in one of the various energy transfer disciplines such as Reiki or Therapeutic Touch. Some individuals possess a great healing ability—developed over a series of lifetimes—and find their way into the traditional medical establishment, or become alternative healers.

The following is a story about a man who discovered healing after looking at past lives. Not only did he awaken new abilities within himself to heal others, he also experienced a spiritual healing of himself.

Tom (a pseudonym) once enjoyed a life of wealth and material pleasure that many would envy. An orthodontist with a thriving practice in Houston, Tom had an income that enabled him to indulge in possessions. A bachelor, he lived in a 3,000-square-foot house and filled it with art. He drove both a Jaguar *and* a Mercedes, wore expensive clothes, and judged everything and everyone around him by appearances. He drank too much, but all in all, he was very happy. Or so he thought.

In 1983, at age forty-three, his life took a radical and drastic downward turn, leading eventually to a series of past-life regressions. Looking into the past opened the door to a transformation of his life.

The genesis of Tom's transformation was a near-fatal car accident that sent him sailing through his windshield. Immediately after the impact, Tom felt himself floating about eight to ten feet above his body, watching the occupants of the car he had hit, who were not seriously injured, attempting to revive him with cardiopulmonary resuscitation. He felt no pain.

As the men worked on his body, Tom's attention was drawn to a bright white light. It was unbelievably brilliant, yet it didn't hurt his eyes. A wonderful sense of well-being permeated him, unlike anything he had ever experienced before. He realized he was moving toward the light, and noticed that there were other people around him moving in the same direction.

Then the frantic attempts of the men to save his life succeeded, and Tom found himself back in his body with a jolt. The sense of well-being was replaced by intense pain. He was keenly disappointed not to have reached the light.

Tom suffered a severe concussion, two fractures in his neck, and one fracture in his back. He was hospitalized, endured a lot of pain, and took a lot of medication. He wore a neck collar for twenty-six months. As a result of his near-death experience, Tom began to look upon life with new appreciation, yet his lifestyle remained largely unchanged.

About two years later, he contracted chronic mononucleosis from one of his young patients, and spent sixteen months in bed. He was forced to sell his practice. He was pumped full of medication, not only for the mononucleosis but also for the lingering effects of the car accident, for at that time he had four different doctors treating him. Disorientation and a severe depression set in, and Tom began to contemplate suicide. He'd always had a strong belief in God, but it was not strong enough to counter his despair.

He tried three times to kill himself. He took thirty-five tablets of an over-the-counter pain medication, far more than a lethal dose, and woke up the following morning without so much as a headache. A few days later, he took forty-five tablets. Nothing happened. The third time, he took fifty-five tablets. To his dismay, he woke up the following morning feeling no ill effects.

Frustrated, Tom cried out loud, "Why can't I do this?"

A voice in his head answered, "This is not open to you."

A few days after his third attempt to kill himself, Tom's sister, aware of his despondency, gave him the telephone number of hypnotherapist Sandee Mac. Tom appreciated his sister's concern but did not intend to call. Yet a few weeks later, he found himself dialing Mac's number, adamant that he see her the next day.

When he had seated himself in her office, Mac asked, "Why are you interested in past-life regression?"

"I'm not," Tom replied. "I really don't know why I'm here."

"What's going on in your life?" she asked.

Tom told her. Mac asked him if he believed in reincarnation. He replied that he had once read a book on Bridey Murphy, and added, "I don't know if I believe in it or not. If that's the way God wants to run things, that's fine. I don't really care one way or the other."

After some discussion, Mac suggested, "Why don't we regress you and see what comes up?"

Tom considered it. "Okay," he agreed, "but I have a very strong belief in God, and if this is going to interfere with that, I don't want to do it."

Mac smiled. "It shouldn't interfere at all. In fact, I think it will surprise you."

Tom underwent weekly sessions for several months, and in each session viewed a number of past lives. He described several that made the greatest impact upon his beliefs and attitudes, and how he changed his life as a result:

The first regression took me back to what I believe was Atlantis. I saw an old man who had the most incredible eyes I had ever seen. They had purity. He was a man who had no deception in his life, no negativity, like I did in my present life. People came to him for help with their problems. He had a strong belief in God and felt that his purpose was to help others. I didn't know it at first, but this man was me.

At the end of the regression, my present self was introduced to my past self so that I could learn from the past life. The old man said to me, "There are a lot of truths, and what is true for one person is not necessarily true for someone else. You have to tell people what is the truth for you and let them determine how it applies to their own lives. You don't make decisions about what you think is true for someone else." I realized that I didn't let people discover their own truths. I was busy deciding what other people needed to know and then telling them that. I thought, "If that's the way I was once, there's no reason why I can't be the same way now."

In my second regression, I was a young woman, again in Atlantis. She had been born blind and with severely deformed limbs, and was treated with healing techniques that we don't have now. Bowls and vats were lined with amethyst or citrine crystals and were filled with water. For treatment, people immersed parts of their bodies in the water.

When I saw the woman, she was in her middle twenties and her limbs had been healed. Even though the power existed to heal her sight, she had chosen to remain blind. She said, "I don't need sight because this way I can see people's souls. I don't need to see their bodies." She was a healer and worked in a circular room divided into areas, each with a different type of bath. She played a musical instrument similar to a harp. Instead of strings, it had crystalline structures. When people stood near it, she moved her hands up and down these crystalline columns, making musical sounds. I could feel the vibration in my hands as her hands moved up and down the prisms.

She said to me, "I've been waiting for you to come back. The most important lesson you need to learn now is that you spend too much time looking at people's physical bodies and making instant decisions. If you can learn to look past the physical body to see the soul, then you will see people as they truly are." I wanted to know how the crystals healed, but she said that was not the important lesson.

Since that session, I look at people differently. I don't pay nearly as much attention to their physical forms—I listen to what they say and try to understand what they feel.

Some of the regressions Tom underwent were in groups with others. In a group session, the regressions were directed to a general theme, such as a life in a specific period of history. During one such regression when participants were directed to find their most powerful past life, Tom found himself once again in Atlantis.

My father was the ruler of a region and I was the second in line to succeed him. I had gotten to know a shaman, a wise man, who lived on the outskirts of town in a cave. He told me, "Every person has every resource they need within themselves. It takes the right person with the right know-how and talent to bring it out." I said, "I don't understand." He said, "You will at the right time, depending on what you choose to do."

He said, "You have two choices: follow your father in succession and have the power of ruling people, or else allow me to give you the ability not only to heal people, but also to teach them that they have the power they need within themselves to do whatever they need to do." I decided that the latter was much more important to me. I didn't care about ruling people, I wanted to help them be rulers of their own lives.

That life helped me see the value in helping others.

In another group session, the theme was to find two past lives, one's poorest and one's richest. Tom found both in the same past life.

I was an American Indian, a young man. At birth I had been given some gifts that made my father, who was the chief of the tribe, jealous. My mother left him in order to protect me. She ran off with a white man who was in love with her. The three of us were ostracized from our respective groups and were very poor. There was no food and no place to stay, and we were hunted and chased wherever we went. The day I died—I was in my teens—we were caught in a little cabin that was on fire because it had been besieged by Indians.

It dawned on me right at the last moment of that life that it was also my richest life. I had a mother who had left everything she knew because of me, and a white man stepfather who loved both of us so much that he had given up everything he had for us.

The Indian boy said to me, "I knew you were coming back to meet me, so that I could tell you that in one life, you had both the poorest and richest life you could imagine." The lesson I learned was that in that life I had everything I needed, even though I didn't have a lot of material things. I had the things that were important. I was extremely happy. Afterward, I couldn't even talk about it. It was overwhelming.

The lesson of self-sufficiency and the richness of life without materialism was presented again to Tom with the help of an animal. The group session's theme was to identify one's animal guardian spirit. In Native American and shamanic cultures, it is believed that everyone has such a guardian spirit, which can be drawn upon for its strengths and attributes. For the shaman, the spirit also functions as a "power animal," which protects and serves him and becomes a virtual alter ego. Animal guardian spirits usually are acquired in vision quests, in which an individual undertakes a lone vigil in the wilderness.

Tom's animal guardian spirit appeared to him as a

white polar bear. He was able to go inside the bear and look out through its eyes. After this experience, he saw that the bear's lesson was that it had everything it needed within itself for sustenance and happiness.

The inner energies and forces released by past-life regressions began to bring about improvements in Tom's life. His attitudes toward materialism changed, and he awakened to an interest in helping others.

In looking back over these regressions, I could see how they all tied together. Our Higher Consciousness picks out the lives we see for a certain reason. I saw how extremely materialistic I'd been, yet I still wasn't happy. So I began to get rid of what I thought I didn't need. Now I have a small, comfortable apartment. I have plants instead of a Mercedes. In fact, I don't even own a car. I'm infinitely more happy than I ever have been in my entire life. I still have some art on the walls, but I don't have to constantly buy things and clothes that I don't need.

I also became very interested in healing. In a lot of other lives, I was involved in medicine or some kind of healing. In a couple of lives, I healed by putting my hands on people. That really intrigued me. I'd heard about laying on of hands, but thought it was church talk. Then I found out about Reiki, which is a hands-on healing technique in which you channel energy. I went through that training and learned how to do it.

I've also learned two other methods of healing, which have involved extensive training. I learned Mahikari, which is a healing system based on a divine revelation given to a Japanese man around

1959 and widely used in some parts of the world. It's similar in principle to Reiki, in that divine light is directed by your hands. The other system is Omega Shakti, which has nine levels of expertise and is taught by only two people in the world, one in California and one in Tibet.

I get a good feeling from doing touch healing that is different from my orthodontics practice. I don't charge for it.

With his orthodontics practice gone, Tom decided to return to school rather than spend another three years establishing another dental practice. He began work on a doctorate in genetic engineering, a subject he had studied in dental school. He also began studying the reputed healing powers of music, and psychotherapy techniques. His life, he said, "just gets better and better, especially when I am helping someone else."

Another transformation for Tom was his discovery and development of his own psychic powers: he learned to astral-project his consciousness out of his body, and to see clairvoyantly.

After he learned how to astral-project, Mac hypnotized him once and suggested that he go to the lower astral plane, where it is believed that suicide victims go upon death. She told him, "You came close to that, and I want you to see what it is like." Tom was horrified by what he encountered.

It was creepy, it was just terrible. It was worse than anything I could imagine. I grew up in small towns hearing about the fiery brimstone of hell and that was bad enough, but this was worse. There was this murky, thick, gray fog I could actually touch—it was like a gel. Big, ugly

261

"things" kept bumping into me. The more agitated I got, the more these big, creepy things bumped into me. It seemed that my agitation attracted them. There was no way out. It just got worse and worse. It was a sensation that I can't really describe. I kept saying, "Can I please leave?" I had only been there a few seconds, but there's no sense of time there. In a few seconds I felt like I'd been there a hundred years.

I've been told that suicide victims stay in this place for as long as they would have lived on earth. I was very thankful I had not succeeded in committing suicide.

The lesson that suicide is counter to divine law was reinforced again when Mac asked Tom to attend a therapy session involving the soul of a suicide victim. A woman had come to Mac, concerned that a friend of hers who had killed herself had not crossed over into the divine light but was stuck somewhere. The woman was anxious to help her friend's soul find peace. Mac hypnotized the woman, then directed her to leave her body so that the soul of the friend could enter, and Mac could talk to her. This was what Tom witnessed:

As the woman went into trance, I could see a beautiful blue aura surrounding her. Sandee said, "I want you to move up and out of your body." I thought the aura would then go away, but it didn't. It raised up about ten or twelve inches from the body and stayed there. Sandee said, "Now I want your friend who committed suicide to come into your body." The minute that soul entered the body and answered, "I'm here," I saw the same thick, gray, gellike fog all over the woman's body.

I got goose bumps and almost jumped out of my skin! Sandee talked to the soul and explained how she should go toward the light. The instant the soul found the light, the gray fog disappeared. The other woman came back into her body and the blue aura returned. I couldn't talk about that for a couple of days. I think God allowed me to see it for a reason, to show me once again that suicide is not acceptable.

Tom's former ambivalence about past-life regression was replaced by a firm conviction of its value.

I still have a lot of questions about reincarnation, but now there's no doubt in my mind that it's true. I have a vivid imagination, but I couldn't make up the things I saw and the feelings I had. My experiences have been *too real not to be real.*

Each time I go to another regression, I know there's a lesson waiting to be learned. I'm excited about it, because I want to learn and grow. The car accident and suicide attempts evidently had a purpose in getting me to where I am now.

I found an astrology chart that a woman did for me in 1980, when I still had a problem with alcohol. She said that my life would make a complete, positive turnaround if I changed direction, especially between the ages of forty-two and forty-six. I was forty-six when I began past-life regression. Since then, I've consulted several psychic readers who didn't know about the car accident. They told me that I had been in a near-fatal collision because I had been following the wrong path, and my guides had tried unsuccessfully to get my attention. The accident apparently was the only way to get it. I did change and started appreciating life more, but I drifted back to the old path, and then I came down with mono.

I don't push anyone about the benefits of past-life regression. When I meet people who are interested, I tell them what it's done for me. It can be a positive building force in one's life.

EPILOGUE

What do all these stories of past-life recall demonstrate? Before we can consider the answers, we must first deal with the issue of "proof" and the matter of religion. From a scientific standpoint, it is doubtful that reincarnation ever will be "proved." While scientific investigation of reincarnation has lent credence to the doctrine among some nonbelievers and has greatly contributed to our understanding of reincarnation, we must look beyond science for the meaning reincarnation has in our lives. Reincarnation is also more than a religious matter. Though some may choose to view it from within the context of religion, this can be limiting since only some religions embrace the concept of reincarnation, and each in different ways.

Coming into contact with past lives can reacquaint us with an ancient, fundamental, and universal truth with which we have lost touch: that all things in the cosmos are interconnected. Past lives help us not only to learn more about ourselves, but also to see ourselves as part of this greater cosmic whole, a whole in constant flux in order to maintain balance. When we see we are irrevocably part of this delicate web, we begin to appreciate how all our actions, physical and mental, no matter how small, affect the greater whole, and how we in turn are affected by the actions of others.

This idea is aptly illustrated in the Hindu and Buddhist analogy of Indra's net. In Hindu mythology, Indra is the primary Vedic god, the lord of warfare, thunder, and storms. He is associated with fertility, and therefore the continuity of life, because of the rain brought by his storms. His knotted net represents all life in the cosmos. Each knot is the life of a sentient being, and is hung with a jewel. The actions in a life shake the jewel, which in turn shakes other jewels, and the resulting light refracts throughout the entire universe.

Past lives open us up to realities that cannot be defined neatly by the five senses. This, too, is an important rediscovery, for it forces us to look beyond the material to the spiritual. In the process, we become closer to the Divine Force.

It is significant that many past-life recalls involve healing: healing of the body and mind, healing of the environment, healing of relationships, healing among the peoples of the planet. That is a direct result of the desperate need for all kinds of healing on this planet. We look around and see great sicknesses—war, disease, pollution, drugs, corruption, abuse. We are shocked to discover that they are no longer someone else's sicknesses and problems, but *our* problems, everyone's.

I do not mean to suggest that looking into past lives provides magic solutions. It does not. The stories presented here demonstrate how past lives can be part of a process of growth, the end result of which is a greater sense of responsibility, for ourselves, for each other, and for all sentient beings.

SELECTED BIBLIOGRAPHY
AND FURTHER READING

BOOKS

The following titles have been grouped according to topic or dominant theme. Some of the titles may fall into two or more categories.

General and Overview; Reincarnation in Religions

Cranston, Sylvia, and Carey Williams. *Reincarnation: A New Horizon in Science, Religion, and Society.* New York: Julian Press, 1984.

Fisher, Joe. *The Case for Reincarnation.* New York: Bantam Books, 1985. First published 1984.

Gallup, George, Jr., with William Proctor. *Adventures in Immortality.* New York: McGraw-Hill Book Co., 1982.

Hall, Manly Palmer. *Reincarnation: The Cycle of Necessity.* Los Angeles: The Philosophical Research Society, 1956.

Hanson, Virginia, and Rosemarie Stewart, eds. *Karma: The Universal Law of Harmony.* 2nd ed. Wheaton, Ill.: The Theosophical Publishing House, 1981.

Head, Joseph, and S.L. Cranston, compilers and editors. *Reincarnation: The Phoenix Fire Mystery.* New York: Julian Press, 1977.

———. *Reincarnation: An East-West Anthology.* Wheaton, Ill.: The Theosophical Publishing House, 1985. First published in 1961.

Selected Bibliography and Further Reading

His Holiness the Fourteenth Dalai Lama, Tenzin Gyatso. *Kindness, Clarity, and Insight*. Ithaca, N.Y.: Snow Lion Publications, 1984.

His Holiness the Dalai Lama of Tibet. *My Land and My People: Memoirs of the Dalai Lama of Tibet*. New York: Potala Corp., 1977, First published 1962.

Hultkrantz, Ake. *The Religions of the American Indians*. Berkeley: University of California Press, 1967.

Kim, Yong Choon. *Oriental Thought*. Totowa, N.J.: Rowman and Littlefield, 1973.

MacGregor, Geddes. *Reincarnation in Christianity*. Wheaton, Ill.: The Theosophical Publishing House, 1978.

Moore, Marcia. *Hypersentience*. New York: Bantam Books, 1977.

Moore, Marcia, and Mark Douglas. *Reincarnation, Key to Immortality*. York Cliffs, Me.: Arcane Publications, 1968.

Sen, K. M. *Hinduism*. Harmondsworth, Middlesex, England: Penguin Books, 1961.

Story, Francis. *Rebirth as Doctrine and Experience*. Kandy, Sri Lanka: Buddhist Publication Society, 1975.

Scientific Investigations of Reincarnation and Related Phenomena

Stevenson, Ian. *Cases of the Reincarnation Type*, Vols. I–IV. Charlottesville, Va.: University Press of Virginia, 1975–1983.

———. *Children Who Remember Previous Lives*. Charlottesville, Va.: University Press of Virginia, 1987.

———. *Twenty Cases Suggestive of Reincarnation*. 2nd ed. Charlottesville, Va.: University Press of Virginia, 1974.

———. *Unlearned Language: New Studies in Xenoglossy*. Charlottesville, Va.: University Press of Virginia, 1984.

———. *Xenoglossy*. Charlottesville, Va.: University Press of Virginia, 1974.

Regression Techniques, Past-Life Discovery, and Past-Life Therapy

Avery, Jeanne. *Astrology and Your Past Lives*. New York: Fireside Books, 1987.

Evans, Jane A. *Twelve Doors to the Soul: Astrology of the Inner Self*. Wheaton, Ill.: The Theosophical Publishing House, 1979.

Fiore, Edith. *You Have Been Here Before*. New York: Ballantine Books, 1978.

Selected Bibliography and Further Reading

Glaskin, G. M. *Windows of the Mind*. New York: Delacorte Press, 1974.

Goldberg, Bruce. *Past Lives, Future Lives*. New York: Ballantine Books, 1982.

Kelsey, Denys, and Joan Grant. *Many Lifetimes*. Garden City, N.Y.: Doubleday, 1967.

Netherton, Morris, and Nancy Shiffrin. *Past Lives Therapy*. New York: Ace Books, 1978.

Talbot, Michael. *Your Past Lives: A Reincarnation Handbook*. New York: Harmony Books, 1987.

Wambach, Helen. *Life before Life*. New York: Bantam Books, 1979.
———. *Reliving Past Lives*. New York: Harper & Row, 1978.

Weiss, Brian L. *Many Lives, Many Masters*. New York: Fireside Books, 1988.

Williston, Glenn, and Judith Johnstone. *Discovering Your Past Lives*. Wellingborough, England: The Aquarian Press, 1988. First published as *Soul Search* in 1983.

Woolger, Roger. *Other Lives, Other Selves*. Garden City, N.Y.: Doubleday, 1987.

Past-Life Accounts

Banerjee, H. N. *Americans Who Have Been Reincarnated*. New York: Macmillan, 1980.

Bernstein, Morey. *The Search for Bridey Murphy*. Revised ed. New York: Avon, 1975. First published 1965.

Clow, Barbara Hand. *Eye of the Centaur*. St. Paul: Llewellyn Publications, 1987.

Cooke, Grace. *The Illumined Ones*. New Lands, England: White Eagle Publishing Trust, 1966.

Cott, Jonathan. *The Search for Omm Sety*. Garden City, N.Y.: Doubleday, 1987.

Ebon, Martin, ed. *Reincarnation in the Twentieth Century*. New York: The World Publishing Co., 1969.

Grant, Joan. *Far Memory*. New York: Harper & Row, 1956.

Guirdham, Arthur. *The Cathars and Reincarnation*. London: Neville Spearman, 1970.

Holzer, Hans. *Born Again*. Garden City, N.Y.: Doubleday, 1970.

Jay, Reverend Carroll E. *Gretchen, I Am*. New York: Wyden Books, 1977.

Lenz, Frederick. *Lifetimes: True Accounts of Reincarnation*. New York: Fawcett Crest, 1977.

Leonardi, Dell. *The Reincarnation of John Wilkes Booth*. Old Greenwich, Conn.: The Devin-Adair Co., 1975.

MacLaine, Shirley. *Out on a Limb*. New York: Bantam Books, 1983.

————. *Dancing in the Light*. New York: Bantam Books, 1985.

Randles, Jenny. *Beyond Explanation?* New York: Bantam Books, 1987.

Stearn, Jess. *The Search for a Soul: Taylor Caldwell's Psychic Lives*. Garden City, N.Y.: Doubleday, 1972.

————. *The Search for the Girl with the Blue Eyes*. Garden City, N.Y.: Doubleday, 1968.

————. *Yoga, Youth, and Reincarnation*. Garden City, N.Y.: Doubleday, 1965.

————. *Soul Mates*. New York: Bantam Books, 1984.

————. *You Were Born Again To Be Together*. New York: Pocket Books, 1976.

Sutphen, Dick. *Past Lives, Future Loves*. New York: Pocket Books, 1978.

Edgar Cayce Readings, Interpretations, and Perspective

Cerminara, Gina. *Many Lives, Many Loves*. New York: William Sloane Assoc., 1963.

————. *Many Mansions*. New York: Signet/New American Library, 1978. First published 1950.

Church, W. H. *Many Happy Returns: The Lives of Edgar Cayce*. San Francisco: Harper & Row, 1984.

Langley, Noel. *Edgar Cayce on Reincarnation*. New York: Castle Books, 1967.

Sparrow, Lynn Elwell. *Reincarnation: Claiming Your Past, Creating Your Future*. San Francisco: Harper & Row, 1988.

Van Auken, John. *Past Lives and Present Relationships*. Virginia Beach, Va.: Inner Vision, 1984.

Woodward, Mary Ann. *Edgar Cayce's Story of Karma*. New York: Coward, McCann & Geoghegan, 1971.

Between-Lives States

Evans-Wentz, W. Y., ed. *The Tibetan Book of the Dead*. 3rd ed. London: Oxford University Press, 1960.

Whitton, Joel L., and Joe Fisher. *Life between Life*. Garden City, N.Y.: Dolphin/Doubleday, 1986.

Atlantis

Cayce, Edgar Evans. *Edgar Cayce on Atlantis*. New York: Warner Books, 1968.

Donnelly, Ignatius. *Atlantis: The Antediluvian World*. New York: Gramercy Publishing, 1985. First published in 1882.

Michell, John. *The New View over Atlantis*. San Francisco: Harper & Row, 1983. First published 1969.

Spence, Lewis. *The History of Atlantis*. Secaucus, N.J.: The Citadel Press, 1968 (reissue).

Westwood, Jennifer, ed. *The Atlas of Mysterious Places*. New York: Weidenfeld & Nicholson, 1987.

ARTICLES

Miscellaneous

"Body and Soul," *Newsweek*. Nov. 7, 1988, pp. 88–97.

Cook, Emily Williams. "Research on Reincarnation-Type Cases: Present Status and Suggestions for Future Research," *Case Studies in Honor of Louisa E. Rhine*. K. Ramakrishna Rao, ed. Jefferson, N.C.: McFarland & Co., 1986.

Dadoo, Pradeep. "Theory of Reincarnation in Terms of Science, Religion, and Yoga," *The Journal of Religion and Psychical Research*. October 1988, Vol. 11, No. 4, pp. 201–202.

———. "Work Done on Reincarnation in Ancient India," *The Journal of Religion and Psychical Research*. January 1989, Vol. 12, No. 1, pp. 7–11.

Gershom, Rabbi Yonassan. "Are Holocaust Victims Returning?" *Venture Inward*. Nov./Dec. 1987, Vol. 3, No. 6, pp. 16–21.

Stevenson, Ian. "Characteristics of Cases of the Reincarnation Type Among the Igbo of Nigeria," *Journal of Asian and African Studies*. 1986, Vol. 21, pp. 204–216.

———. "The Explanatory Value of the Idea of Reincarnation," *The Journal of Nervous and Mental Disease*. 1977, Vol. 164, No. 5, pp. 305–326.